Word, Liturgy, Charity

Word, Liturgy, Charity

The Diaconate in the U.S. Catholic Church, 1968–2018

Center for Applied Research
in the Apostolate

LEXINGTON BOOKS
Lanham • Boulder • New York • London

Published by Lexington Books
An imprint of The Rowman & Littlefield Publishing Group, Inc.
4501 Forbes Boulevard, Suite 200, Lanham, Maryland 20706
www.rowman.com

Unit A, Whitacre Mews, 26-34 Stannary Street, London SE11 4AB

Copyright © 2018 The Rowman & Littlefield Publishing Group, Inc.

Quotations from *Permanent Deacons in the United States: Guidelines on Their Formation and Ministry* (1971); *Permanent Deacons in the United States: Guidelines on Their Formation and Ministry* (1985); and *National Directory for the Formation, Ministry, and Life of Permanent Deacons in the United States* (2005) are used with permission.

All rights reserved. No part of this book may be reproduced in any form or by any electronic or mechanical means, including information storage and retrieval systems, without written permission from the publisher, except by a reviewer who may quote passages in a review.

British Library Cataloguing in Publication Information Available

Library of Congress Cataloging-in-Publication Data Available

ISBN: 978-1-4985-7626-0 (cloth : alk. paper)
ISBN: 978-1-4985-7628-4 (pbk. : alk. paper)
ISBN: 978-1-4985-7627-7 (electronic)

∞™ The paper used in this publication meets the minimum requirements of American National Standard for Information Sciences—Permanence of Paper for Printed Library Materials, ANSI/NISO Z39.48-1992.

Printed in the United States of America

Contents

Acknowledgments		vii
Introduction		ix
1	What is the Purpose of the Diaconate? A Normative Description of the Diaconate *Michal J. Kramarek*	1
2	How is the Diaconate Changing? Trends in the Presence and Ministry of Deacons *Mary L. Gautier*	29
3	Who are the Deacons? Demographic Characteristics of Deacons *Mary L. Gautier*	45
4	What Does It Take to Become a Deacon? Deacons' Vocation and Formation *Michal J. Kramarek*	59
5	What Do the Deacons Do? The Ministries of Deacons *Thu T. Do, LHC, and Michal J. Kramarek*	81
6	Is It Satisfying to Be a Deacon? Measuring Satisfaction among Deacons *Jonathon L. Wiggins*	101
7	What Does It Mean to Be a Deacon's Wife? The Diaconate from the Spouse's Perspective *Mark M. Gray*	119

| 8 | Where Do Deacons Fit within the Diocese? The Diaconate in the Church's Structures
Thomas P. Gaunt, SJ | 137 |

References 151

Index 157

About the Contributors 163

Acknowledgments

This book would not have been possible without the cooperation, support, and guidance of many people. In particular, we wish to thank the National Association of Diaconate Directors (NADD) for their guidance and support throughout this project, which would never have happened without them. Foremost among the leadership at NADD, we are indebted to Deacon Gerald DuPont, whose vision, patience, and persistence guided this process from beginning to end. Deacon DuPont also arranged the majority of the funding for the project, in his role as Director of the Diaconate for the Archdiocese of Galveston-Houston, and through his contacts there. We acknowledge the foundations and deacons of the Archdiocese of Galveston-Houston, whose donations made this study possible. We are grateful to the U.S. Conference of Catholic Bishops' Secretariat of Clergy, Consecrated Life and Vocations, and to the two executive directors of that office—Fr. Shawn McKnight and Fr. Ralph O'Donnell—for graciously funding part of the research and for providing sage and helpful counsel at various points along the way.

We are grateful to Deacon William Ditewig, executive director emeritus of the USCCB Secretariat for the Diaconate, who initiated an annual study of Diocesan Offices of the Permanent Diaconate while he was at the USCCB. We incorporate findings from these ten annual studies throughout this book. Deacon Ditewig also graciously agreed to read an early version of chapter 1, and his insightful critique strengthened the chapter substantially.

Two other CARA staff also deserve acknowledgement. Felice Goodwin transcribed the audiotapes from the focus groups of deacons' wives and of bishops. She also entered the data from the paper surveys that were returned to CARA. Sr. Florence Emurayeveya, EHJ, a sister-scholar-in-residence at CARA for six months in 2017–2018, provided a review of the literature on deacons for this book. Sister also analyzed and coded the open-ended comments from deacons that were provided on the surveys of deacons.

Finally, we are deeply grateful to the bishops, diaconate directors, deacons' wives, and deacons who responded to our surveys and other requests for data. They shared many aspects of the diaconate with us and enriched the study with their comments. We hope that we have fairly represented their opinions and experiences here.

Any mistakes are the sole responsibility of the authors, all of whom are CARA research staff.

Introduction

This book had its genesis in a conversation between three interested parties in November, 2012, during the annual meeting of the U.S. Conference of Catholic Bishops, in Baltimore, Maryland. Fr. Shawn McKnight, then executive director of the USCCB Secretariat of Clergy, Consecrated Life and Vocations (now Bishop Shawn McKnight of Jefferson City), Deacon Gerald DuPont, then president of the National Association of Diaconate Directors (now president emeritus of NADD and president of the International Diaconate Centre), and Dr. Mary Gautier, senior research associate at the Center for Applied Research in the Apostolate (CARA, at Georgetown University) gathered over breakfast to discuss the possibilities for a major national research study on the diaconate in the United States. The idea was to design a multi-modal research study, based on two previous national studies of the diaconate that had been commissioned and published by the USCCB in 1981 and in 1996. This present study would be national in scope and would draw insights from deacons, deacons' wives, diocesan directors of the diaconate, and bishops, as was done in the two previous studies. This would allow a comparison of findings from the three points in time to explore trends in the diaconate in the United States over the course of the first fifty years since its restoration in 1968.

After a series of follow-up conversations to secure funding for the project and ensure support from all parties, CARA was commissioned by NADD and the USCCB to conduct a comprehensive national study of the permanent diaconate in the United States and deliver a monograph of its findings in time for the 2018 Diaconate Congress, celebrating the 50th anniversary of the renewal of the Order of Diaconate as a permanent ordained ministry of the Catholic Church in the United States. What follows is the fruits of this original conversation.

2017 NATIONAL STUDY OF THE DIACONATE

The 2017 national study of the diaconate involved four major components:

- A national survey of the Office of the Permanent Diaconate in dioceses and eparchies in the United States. The survey instrument was expanded from a survey of the Office of the Permanent Diaconate that CARA has been conducting annually for the USCCB since 2006, and consisted of 149 questions and two boxes for open-ended comments about the impact of the diaconate in the diocese and the director's perception of the future of the diaconate in the next twenty-five years. The survey could be completed either online or on paper. CARA completed data collection in April 2017, and received information from 152 of the 193 dioceses and eparchies whose bishops and eparchs belong to the USCCB, for a 79 percent overall completion rate.
- A national survey of U.S. deacons. In collaboration with executive leadership at NADD, CARA designed a survey for deacons, consisting of 176 questions and one box for open-ended comments about what deacons would like to see improved in the diaconate. The survey was translated into Spanish and was programmed into an online format, so that deacons could respond either online or on paper. Using lists of deacons provided by 25 dioceses as well as a comprehensive national list of deacons from *The Official Catholic Directory*, CARA compiled an exhaustive list of 16,454 deacons to survey. In September 2017, CARA e-mailed an invitation to the survey to 3,407 deacons for whom an e-mail address had been provided and mailed the survey to an additional 13,047 deacons with no e-mail address. All bounced e-mails were followed up with a mailed survey. A total of 349 mailed surveys were returned by the post office as invalid and another 17 deacons were reported by a family member to be deceased, thus reducing the population to 16,088. By the cutoff in November 2017, CARA received a total of 3,166 valid responses to the survey, for a margin of sampling error of ±1.6 percent. In other words, assuming random distribution of non-responses, we can be confident (with 95 percent certainty) that the response to any particular item in the survey would be within 1.6 percentage points (either above or below) of the response presented here if the entire population of deacons had responded to the survey.
- Two focus groups of deacons' wives. CARA conducted two focus groups of deacon's wives at the NADD Conference in April 2017. A total of 22 wives participated in the focus groups, which were facilitated by a CARA researcher and guided by a protocol developed by CARA and NADD. Each focus group lasted approximately 1.5 hours and was audiotaped and then transcribed by CARA.

- One focus group of bishops was arranged by Fr. Ralph O'Donnell, executive director of the USCCB Secretariat of Clergy, Consecrated Life and Vocations. This focus group took place during the USCCB summer meeting in Indianapolis in June 2017. A total of eight bishops participated in the focus group, which was facilitated by a CARA researcher and guided by a protocol developed by CARA and NADD. The focus group lasted approximately half an hour and was audiotaped and transcribed by CARA.

OTHER NATIONAL STUDIES OF DEACONS USED IN THIS BOOK

In addition to the 2017 National Study of the Diaconate described above, we also compared the findings, where applicable, to several other national studies of U.S. deacons. These studies include:

- A national telephone poll of a representative sample of 804 permanent deacons that was conducted by CARA in February 2001. The 2001 CARA Deacon Poll included a variety of questions about the background and demographic characteristics of deacons, their ministry profiles, their attitudes about service, and satisfaction with their role as a deacon. Interviewing was conducted using a list of permanent deacons from *The Official Catholic Directory*. Following standard assumptions of statistical inference, a sample size of 804 provides a margin of error of approximately ±3.5 percent. In other words, assuming true random sampling, the characteristics of deacons in the CARA Deacon Poll can be assumed to be within 3.5 percentage points of the characteristics of all U.S. deacons.
- In 1993, the Bishops' Committee on the Permanent Diaconate commissioned a major national study of the diaconate in the United States, published in 1996 as *A National Study on the Permanent Diaconate of the Catholic Church in the United States: 1994–1995*. The study involved four national surveys: a sample of 3,073 deacons (margin of error approximately ±3 percent), a survey of deacons' wives (using 1,850 names taken from the returned deacon surveys, which yielded a response of 64 percent, or 1,194 surveys from wives), a survey of the supervisors/directors of deacons (again using 1,719 names selected from the returned deacon surveys, which yielded a response of 31 percent, or 533 surveys returned by supervisors of deacons), and a survey of parish lay leaders (using 1,687 names of parish council members selected from the returned deacon surveys, which yielded a response of 34 percent, or 581 surveys returned).

- In 1981, the Bishops' Committee on the Permanent Diaconate published the results of the first ever national study of the diaconate in the United States as *A National Study of the Permanent Diaconate in the United States*. This study was conducted by the U.S. Bishops' Office of Research and involved four surveys: a sample of 1,506 deacons (out of a total of 2,338 sent, for a 64 percent response rate), a survey of the wives of deacons (sent to 1,282 wives, with 696 returned, for a 54 percent response), a survey of the supervisors of deacons (sent to 1,296 supervisors and completed by 635, for a 54 percent response), and a survey of 285 active bishops (with a response from 196, or 69 percent).

These national studies all informed this 2017 study and we are grateful for the work that went into them.

Chapter One

What is the Purpose of the Diaconate?
A Normative Description of the Diaconate
Michal J. Kramarek

The aim of this chapter is to provide a brief depiction of the purpose of the permanent diaconate (from here on referred to simply as diaconate) based on the normative documents of the Church (as opposed to descriptive characterization based on empirical evidence). This exploration is organized into three parts. The first part provides a summary of deacons' seven main functions which aggregates and categorizes various specific purposes that deacons serve. The second part looks in more detail into those specific purposes in chronological order according to three groups of sources: scripture and its interpretations, historical documents informing Church tradition, and normative documents of the Church issued by the Holy See and by the U.S. bishops during and after the Second Vatican Council. The third part of the chapter provides some context by exploring similarities and differences between norms guiding the diaconate and those guiding contemporary American philanthropy.

SUMMARY OF DEACONS' FUNCTIONS

The normative documents of the Church depict several different purposes of the diaconate. Those purposes can be categorized and aggregated into seven main functions: complementary, symbolic, unitive, sacramental, institutional, organizational, and sanctioned. Unlike competing interpretations of the same document that cancel each other out, the functions listed here complement each other. Each of the functions is defined and described below.

Complementary Function

The purpose of the diaconate is to complement the two other orders in the sacred hierarchy. According to Campbell, "a deacon is ordained and a member of the hierarchy. A deacon is part of the constitution of the church instituted by the will of Christ. The fullness of the church includes the deacon, and the deacon is a part of that fullness of the realization of the church by divine institution. Therefore, a church without the diaconate is a church that is incompletely manifested to the people" (2006: 20).

This understanding of the diaconate's purpose is used to explain why the order was restored at the Vatican Council II. As Pope Paul VI (1968) states, the purpose of reestablishing a diaconate is to complete the hierarchy of sacred orders.

As such, the complementary function of the diaconate derives directly from the tradition. Therefore, in broader perspective, the purpose of the diaconate is in maintaining the tradition. This is not only a function of the diaconate as an order, but a function of individual deacons, too. According to Pope St. John Paul II (1995), "fidelity to Catholic tradition should mark a deacon's ministry."

Notably, this tradition—while continuous—is evolving. There is some evidence that, in the apostolic Church, bishops, presbyters, and deacons were equal in the way they complemented each other (Barnett 1995). The relationship between them could be likened to the branches growing from the same vine (John 15:5). St. Polycarp writes about deacons as "servants of God and of Christ and not of men" (Richardson 1995: 133). As the Church developed strategies to serve the increasingly numerous body of the faithful, the diaconate was clearly seen as subservient to the episcopate, while the relationship between the diaconate and the presbyterate was more ambiguous. By the Middle Ages, the three sacred orders complemented each other in a hierarchical way with the diaconate being the lowest order.

The contemporary documents of the Church tend to build from this more recent tradition. According to Pope Paul VI, all deacons' "functions must be carried out in perfect communion with the bishop and with his presbytery, that is to say, under the authority of the bishop and of the priests who are in charge of the care of souls in that place" (1967: §23). According to the *Catechism of the Catholic Church*, "Catholic doctrine, expressed in the liturgy, the Magisterium, and the constant practice of the Church, recognizes that there are two degrees of ministerial participation in the priesthood of Christ: the episcopacy and the presbyterate; the diaconate is intended to help and serve them" (1997: §1554). According to the Congregation for Bishops, the diaconate is "a service to the episcopate and to the presbyterate, to which the order of deacons is joined by bonds of obedience and communion, according to canonical discipline" (2004: §92).

Notably, two caveats should be added regarding those norms. First, some exceptions may exist to the authority of bishops and priests over deacons, for example, in case of deacons who are members of religious orders. Second, just like the functions of deacons in relationship to other orders changed in the past, they are likely to be continually shaped by various forces in the future. Those forces may derive, for example, from the growing shortage of priests or from the disparities between the needs of the Church and individual callings of deacons. While those forces may lead to tensions among the three orders, they do not have to be interpreted as an intrinsically negative thing. According to Murnion, there "will be, in the wonderful flowering of ministerial consciousness, a constant tension between individual call and ecclesial ministry, and this tension should be maintained" (1985: 71).

Symbolic Function

The purpose of the diaconate is to symbolize Christ the Servant and to symbolize the inner connection between different areas of the Church's life. This understanding of the diaconate's role is deeply rooted in the tradition. For example, according to St. Ignatius of Antioch (first century), the office of the deacon is nothing other than "the ministry of Jesus Christ, who was with the Father before all ages and has been manifested in the final time" (*Ad Magnesios,* VI, 1: Funk, *Patres Apostolici* 1, 235 in Pope Paul VI 1972) and the deacons "who are ministers of the mysteries of Jesus Christ should please all in every way; for they are not servants of food and drink, but ministers of the Church of God" (*Ad Trallianos,* II, 3: ibid., 245 in Pope Paul VI 1972).

According to Pope St. John Paul II (1985), individual deacons are supposed to personify Christ the servant of the Father by participating in the threefold function, while the office of the diaconate is supposed to contribute to the birth of the Church as a reality of communion, service, and mission.

Overall, the symbolic function of the diaconate can be considered more important than the other functions. According to Barnett, the diaconate's "primary significance does not lie in any of its functions, whether pastoral, charitable/societal, or liturgical. The origin of the diaconate and its development in the first centuries reveals above all the deacon as symbol par excellence of the Church's ministry. The deacon illuminates the indelible character of service Christ put on his ministry and of servant on those who minister. He is the embodiment of the first principle of this ministry: sent and serve" (1995: 137).

Unitive Function

According to the unitive function, *the purpose of the diaconate is to serve God, the people of God and the Church in the diakonia of the Gospel that unites ministerial areas of word, sacrament, and pastoral service* (*Catechism of the Catholic Church*: §875, 1588, 1596). *Diakonia* can be translated as "service," or as "waiting" (as in "waiting on tables"). It is not a function exclusively attributed to the diaconate. According to Searle, *diakonia* is "a constitutive part of the life of the Church and of her mission, which is to say that it is an indispensable part of the Christian life of all the baptized. (. . .) a believer who does not practice 'diakonia' is not a Christian" (1985: 94).

In this context, the unitive function of deacons and of all the faithful is closely related. According to Hypher, "the restoration of the sacramental order of diaconate can only make sense and can only succeed within the context of a thorough-going renewal of the 'diakonia' of the whole Church. In view of the strength of the renewal of the lay apostolate, the ordaining of deacons without the renewal of 'diakonia' can only end up as a frustrating clericalized irrelevance" (1985: 41).

While deacons may perform a wide range of functions, those functions should be balanced between the three ministerial areas of word, sacrament, and pastoral service (Bishops' Committee on the Diaconate 1971). The ministry of word focuses on proclaiming and illustrating the word of God (Pope St. John Paul II 1985), proclaiming the Scriptures as well as instructing and exhorting the people (Congregation for Catholic Education 1998). The ministry of liturgy or sacrament focuses on administering the selected sacraments (Pope St. John Paul II 1985) and the sacramentals (Congregation for Bishops 2004), as well as assisting in various liturgical functions (Kwatera 2005). Finally, the ministry of charity or service can be understood as "the ministry of love and justice" (Bishops' Committee on the Diaconate 1985) that focuses on carrying out works of charity and assistance (Congregation for Catholic Education 1998) by serving as a community animator, by serving in ecclesial life (Pope St. John Paul II 1985), as well as by serving in those areas related to the exercise of charity and the administration of goods (Congregation for Bishops 2004).

Historically, the purpose of the diaconate might not always have included ministry in all three of those areas. While most research does not seem to question deacons' ministry in all three areas, according to Barnett (1995), preaching was not among the deacon's functions in the early Church. Furthermore, the extent of functions performed in the other two areas differed from the current practices (as explained in the following section).

The contemporary relationship among the three areas of ministry can be understood in various, albeit complementary ways. According to the Congregation for Catholic Education, the three areas are not equal in that "the diaconal ministry has its point of departure and arrival in the Eucharist, and cannot be reduced to simple social service" (1998: §9). According to the

Bishops' Committee on the Liturgy, the ministry of charity and justice "is always related to the word and the altar" (1979: 39). According to the Congregation for the Clergy, the three areas are interconnected: "the ministry of the word leads to ministry at the altar, which in turn prompts the transformation of life by the liturgy, resulting in charity" (1998: §39).

According to Searle (1985), the three ministries should be approached as one. As he states, there "is some truth in the exaggeration that Christ came to abolish the distinction between worship and life, between cult and social concern" (1985: 96). Hypher concurs by stating that the three areas of ministry "are different aspects of the one proclamation of the Gospel. Put briefly, liturgy without word and charity becomes superstition or escapism; word without liturgy and charity becomes arid, intellectual philosophizing; and charity without word and liturgy becomes social work and sheer activism" (1985: 40).

Finally, according to Campbell (2006), the balance between the three areas of ministry is to some extent determined by changing needs and the individual predispositions of each individual deacon. However, he notes that every deacon should be prepared to undertake ministry in each of the three areas (Bishops' Committee on the Diaconate 2005).

Sacramental Function

The purpose of the diaconate is to exercise sacramental grace rather than to perform specific functions, because none of those functions are reserved exclusively to the deacons (Pope Paul VI 1965). In this perspective, the deacon's identity is based upon: "the invitation of the Spirit, the manifestation and realization of this call through sacramental ordination for the benefit of the universal Church, the special fraternal sharing of accountability for the kingdom with all ordained ministers, the acceptance by the community he is called to serve, and the complete personal commitment of self to serve in the name of Christ and His Church" (Bishops' Committee on the Diaconate 1971: §14).

In other words, the purpose of a diaconate can be more properly defined in terms of who he is rather than of what he does. According to Pope St. John Paul II (1995), the purpose of deacons is "to be a person open to all, ready to serve people, generous in promoting just social causes, avoiding attitudes or positions which could make him appear to show favoritism."

While the functions that a deacon performs do not make him a deacon, the functions that a deacon performs make the functions diaconal. According to the Congregation for Bishops, while functions assigned to deacons "may also be performed by the lay faithful, they are always diaconal when performed by a deacon in the name of the Church, and sustained by the grace of the sacrament" (2004: §92).

Institutional Function

The institutionalization of ministry by diaconal ordination serves the purpose of strengthening this ministry. This function focuses on the relationship between the deacon and his office. In this context, the purpose of the institution of the diaconate is to give authority to those who were "sent," and the purpose of deacons is to exercise this authority by performing works of "service" just like Christ was "sent" (Luke 4:16–21; Luke 4:43; Matthew 15:24; Mark 9:37) to "serve" (Matthew 20:28; Mark 10:45) (Barnett 1995).

In Church tradition, the origin of this function can be traced to the early second century (around the time of the first letter to Timothy) when the diaconate became an office in a technical sense (Barnett 1995). During the Middle Ages, when the diaconate largely disappeared as a permanent state of life, so did its institutional function, even though other functions (such as unitive and organizational functions) continued to be carried out, being taken over by others (in particular, by the religious orders). In this sense, the recent "revival of the diaconate has been revival of a ministerial status, more than of ministry" (Murnion 1985: 72).

On an individual level, institutionalizing a ministry (i.e., performing a ministry as a deacon as opposed to a layman) makes this ministry stronger, because diaconal ordination turns a "servant" lay minister into a "servant-leader" deacon (Hubbard 1985). The ordination into the diaconate strengthens those men who *de facto* already carried out the ministry and improves their effectiveness (Pope Paul VI 1965). The ordination also affirms deacons in already carried out ministries and expands the scope of ministerial opportunities (Murnion 1985).

Notably, the institutional function of the diaconate has to be treated as subservient to the above-described sacramental function. The relationship between those two functions is reflected in the evolution of contemporary thinking about the purpose of the diaconate. In 1966, Rahner contended that there are many lay people in the Church who carry out services that are classically associated with the deacon. The purpose of the deacon is to better recognize them in the community by giving them the title of the office they already fulfill. Himes (1985) criticized this view, because, among other things, "it implies that all those who are functioning in any ministry of service within the Church are *ipso facto* 'anonymous deacons' who can and, Rahner argues, should be ordained to that office, thereby utterly destroying any ministry of the laity'" (1985: 63) excluding the ministry of women. In his later work, Rahner revised his views to acknowledge that the role of deacon cannot be exercised outside the sacrament of Holy Orders and that "a sacramental commission is reasonable and productive of grace" (1974: 199).

Organizational Function

The purpose of the diaconate is to increase the Church's organizational capacity to address diverse needs. In the Scripture, the organizational function can be traced to the appointment of the Seven (Acts 6:1–15). According to Fuller and Westberg (2006), the Seven were *de facto* leaders of the "Hellenists" prior to their appointment. In an effort to better organize increasingly numerous and diverse Church community in general and to avoid a potential split between "Hellenists" and "Hebrews" in particular, the apostles formally appointed the Seven to what is now considered the diaconate.

The importance of the organizational function is apparent in the documents reestablishing the diaconate after the Second Vatican Council. According to the U.S. Bishops' Conference, the purpose of establishing the diaconate in the United States was to enlist a new group of devout and competent men in the active ministry, extend needed services to the faithful, provide the presence of the Church in areas of secular life as well as areas where few or no priests are available, and improve the Church's ability to adapt to the rapidly changing needs of the society (Ditewig 2006).

Currently, the organizational function finds a number of different expressions. First, the diaconal office increases the Church's presence in communities where there is a shortage of priests through greater local presence and through decentralization. Deacons can help small or remote communities "obliged to live in the Diaspora, cut off from any other group of Christians because of differences in religion, geographical distance, or political circumstances" (Suenens 1985: 48).

Decentralization allows for the multiplication of places of cult and of meeting as well as for creation of smaller, more human groups that "can restore a family atmosphere, a fraternal warmth, to groups suffering from overgrowth" (Suenens 1985: 49). Decentralization makes it possible to "divide the parish community, which suffers from overgrowth, into smaller units, where a sense of community can be nurtured and fostered" (Hubbard 1985: 84). Decentralization also helps the faithful in densely populated areas to rediscover "the intimate and family dimensions of the Church" (Suenens 1985: 48).

Another way the diaconal office serves the Church is by increasing Her presence in missionary areas, and in widely dispersed communities (Pope Paul VI 1967). The diaconate also provides "the opportunity for sacramentally supported and formally recognized indigenous leadership, especially in black and Hispanic communities" (Murnion 1985: 71).

The diaconate also allows the Church to reach deeper into society. The diaconate permits "a greater and more direct presence of sacred ministers in areas such as family, work, schools, etc." (Pope St. John Paul II 1993). As such, the diaconate may help promote and sustain the apostolic works of laymen (Pope Paul VI 1967: V). The diaconate connects sacramental ministry with the married state and the celibate state. Consequently, it brings "more closely into the conduct of sacraments the secular life in which the sacraments share" (Murnion 1985: 72). And, the diaconate also aides the expansion of "ministries into many areas where the challenge, liberation, and healing of Christ otherwise might not have been felt" (Murnion 1985: 72).

Notably, the diaconate improves the Church's capacity to serve the needs of the faithful, not only by increasing the number of those in official ministry but also by increasing the quality of ministry, especially in new areas of the Church's activity. According to Hypher, "[a] properly restored diaconate, where deacons are clearly seen to be part of the normal church community, will allow for professionalism and expertise in areas of diaconal work—essential in our scientific society, facing problems of technological importance" (1985: 43).

Finally, the diaconate has the ability to bolster the Church's capacity to address as yet unforeseen problems. Since the theological understanding of the diaconate is somewhat open, the purpose of the diaconate is relatively flexible and can be adapted to changing circumstances (Hypher 1985). In this context, the diaconate might be defined as a disposal ministry of the bishop, for example, "the deacon might inaugurate 'ad hoc' programs, responding to particular concerns like drug addiction, poor ministry, immigrants, migrant workers, etc. He could research the need, experiment with pastoral approaches, and then, as the picture becomes clearer, turn the ministry over to priests, religious, or laity as seems most appropriate" (Hubbard 1985: 83).

Sanctioned Function

The purpose of the diaconate can be defined by the specific functions listed in the normative documents of the Church. The list of those functions is wide, open-ended, and not exclusive of laity and priesthood (Bishops' Committee on the Diaconate 1971). Furthermore, the assignment of specific functions is subject to the approval by local Church authorities. Nonetheless, those functions offer practical examples of various purposes deacons may be expected to serve.

Arguably, the sanctioned functions are most explicit in regard to deacons' activities in the liturgical area. For example, six out of eleven functions of the diaconate listed in the apostolic letter which established canonical norms for the diaconate focus on the liturgy, sacraments, and sacramentals (Pope Paul VI: 1967).

In comparison to bishops and priests, deacons are not allowed to celebrate the Eucharist or hear confessions. On the other hand, deacons "are the only clerics who may become actively involved in political parties, assume public offices, direct labor unions" (*Code of Canon Law*: can. 288 in Kraus 1997: 44).

Deacons are also granted functions in the areas of preaching the word (can. 610) including, for example, giving homilies (can. 614), participating in the celebration of the Divine Liturgy (can. 699) and administration of sacraments (can. 677, 709).

The diaconal functions regarding charity are relatively open. Those functions include, for example, promoting and sustaining the apostolic activities of laymen, carrying out the duties of charity and of administration, as well as works of social assistance (Pope Paul VI 1967). U.S. Bishops' Committee on the Permanent Diaconate (1971) offers guidelines related to diaconal service in four types of communities: the black community, the Spanish-speaking community, the rural community, as well as on college and university campuses.

Beyond specifying particular functions, the documents of the Church are explicit about the subservient role of the deacons to bishops and priests. For example, deacons are obliged to submit written material concerning faith or morals before its publication [can. 823, §1] to the judgement of their Ordinaries, and to obtain the permission of the Ordinary before writing in publications that habitually attack the Catholic religion or good morals (Congregation for the Clergy 1998: §26).

DEACONS' PURPOSE IN THE SCRIPTURE

Deacon's function can be explored in more detail by investigating in chronological order the changing practices and interpretations regarding the role of deacons. The point of departure in this investigation is in the Scripture. Some authors attempt to reconstruct the purpose of the diaconate from a semantic analysis of the words "deacon" and/or diakonia. However, this approach appears to have considerable limitations. The noun "diakonos" appears thirty times in the *New Testament*. According to Barnett (1995), the words "diakonos," "diakonia," and "diakoneō" are used, for example, to describe the works of Christ (Luke 22:27), the Twelve (Mark 9:35), St. Paul (Colossians 1:23), women of Galilee (Mark 15:41), and Martha (Luke 10:40), but also of the servants of Satan (2 Corinthians 11:15).

While the diaconate does not appear to be well defined and uniformly practiced, the Scripture offers insights about its origins as well as information that was used by the Apostolic Fathers and others as the cornerstone in developing an increasingly well-defined institution.

Appointments in the Old Testament

In the Old Testament, the predecessor to the institution of the diaconate can be found in the appointment of Levites by God to serve Aaron and the priests (*Catechism of the Catholic Church* 1997: §1543). The role of the Levites was to serve the priests while the priests attend to their obligations related to the sanctuary and the altar (Numbers 18). Levites served as door-keepers, chanters, administrators, and custodians of loaves and vessels. One of the specific duties (and a reward) of the Levites was the collection of tithes.

Current literature tends to disagree on the relationship between the offices of Levites and deacons. For example, Echlin (1971) observes that the similarities between Levites and deacons are striking. On the other hand, Barnett (1995) dismisses the proposition that Levites are a prototype for deacons. This later view appears to be much more prevalent among contemporary theologians.

Example of Christ

In the New Testament, the purpose of the diaconate can be based on the role model of Christ as the "one who serves," on the teachings of Christ, and on the appointments bestowed on specific individuals. The scripture shows Christ as the servant "par excellence" who lived totally at the service of God, for the good of men (Congregation for Catholic Education 1998): He declared that He was anointed "to bring good news to the poor," as well as "to proclaim release to the captives and recovery of sight to the blind, to let the oppressed go free" (Luke 4:16–22).

Christ explicitly qualified His actions as diakonia: He "came not to be served but to serve, and to give his life a ransom for many" (Matthew 20:28; Mark 10:45), He declared Himself as the one who serves (Luke 22:27), He washed the disciples' feet (John 13:1–17), and He "emptied himself, taking the form of a slave, being born in human likeness. And being found in human form, he humbled himself and became obedient to the point of death" (Philippians 2:7–8). The death on the cross can be considered the greatest act of diakonia and a starting point in defining what is the service that a deacon should strive to offer (Campbell 2006).

Teachings in the New Testament

The purpose of the diaconate can be interpreted not only from actions but also from the teachings of Christ, who instructed His followers to "love one another" (John 13:34–35), to serve their slaves (Luke 12:37), to seek greatness by becoming servants (Matthew 20:26), to sell "possessions, and give the money to the poor (. . .); then come, follow" Him (Matthew 19:16–22). The changing interpretation of the last teaching (about the rich young men who went away sorrowful) offers a good example of the challenge in applying the Scripture to practice. For instance, Athanasius (third to fourth century) interprets the parable literally and uses it as an explanation and justification of St. Anthony's decision to give away all the family property to the poor (Athanasius n.d.).

St. Augustine (fourth to fifth century) describes the choice set before the young man as a transaction involving earthly things passed between the young man and the poor, as well as the heavenly reward promised to the young man by God in return (St. Augustine n.d.).

St. John Chrysostom (fourth to fifth century) focuses on the importance of sharing with the neighbor out of the concern for the condition of this neighbor, and not only out of concern for the salvation of the young man (St. John Chrysostom n.d.).

St. Thomas Aquinas (thirteenth century) among other things, points out that Jesus' reply could have been specifically intended for the young man and does not have to imply a general call to the poor life. He observes that the young man might have been advised to give away his property not for the sake of securing his place in heaven, but for the sake of his neighbor. He concludes that whoever gives away his possessions has a treasure in heaven and becomes of heaven (St. Thomas Aquinas n.d.).

In a contemporary reflection about the meaning of the parable, Johnson states that "[r]eading Luke-Acts, we could conclude that only those economically poor are really part of God's kingdom, and on that basis would take literally the command to leave all possessions to follow Jesus. If we did that, however, we would not be able to fulfill another, equally serious, commandment, namely to give alms to the poor. Nor could we give alms if we followed another apparent prescription, that Christians join all their possessions in a community of goods. The mandates appear to cancel each other out" (2006: 7).

Appointments in the New Testament

In addition to the teachings of Christ, the purpose of the diaconate can be interpreted based on the appointments (or duties) bestowed on specific individuals in the New Testament. In various interpretations, those individuals included sister Phoebe, "a benefactor of many" (Romans 16:1–2), Epaphroditus, a minister to St. Paul (Philippians 2:25 and 30), Timothy, a coworker of

St. Paul (1 Thessalonians 3:2), Epaphras, St. Paul's beloved "fellow servant" and "a faithful minister of Christ" (Colossians 1:7), and Tychicus, "beloved brother, a faithful minister, and a fellow servant in the Lord" (Colossians 4:7 and Ephesians 6:21).

Notably, the most prominent example of those appointments is the choice of the seven men for the ministry of tables for the benefit of the Greek-speaking widows (Acts 6:1–15), so that the twelve apostles could remain focused on the ministry of the word. The Church interprets these passages as the Seven being ordained deacons (e.g., Pope Paul VI 1967, Pope St. John Paul II 1985). St. Irenaeus (second century) goes as far as to says that St. Stephen (one of the seven) "was the first chosen for diaconal service by the Apostles" (Adversus Haereses 4.15. 1, PG 7:1013).

However, some disagree with this interpretation. For instance, according to Brown, "[i]t can be seriously questioned whether this incident narrated in the Acts is, in fact, a reference to the institution of the order of the diaconate. Reservations arise not only from the fact that the Seven are not referred to with the title 'diakonoi,' but also because, contrary to the narrative, several of the Seven later on appeared to be engaged in the ministry of the word, and Philip is recorded as having baptized. It is impossible to detect whether this inconsistency originates in Luke or in the practice of the primitive Church" (Ziegler 1985: 5–6).

Hypher states that "it is not sound exegesis or theology to build one's understanding of the nature and meaning of the ordained diaconate around the election of the Seven (nowhere called deacons) in Acts 6. This text is helpful in development of ministry in the New Testament as a response to immediate practical problems, in this case, the failure of church leadership to provide for a fair distribution of alms to Hellenist Christian widows. The text is not about job demarcation between deacons and apostles or presbyters, for later passages in Acts show that the Seven begin to take on the same sort of oversight and preaching role, on behalf of Hellenistic community, as some of the apostles exercised for the Hebrew Christian community. The text, therefore, does not help us in understanding the role and function of what are later called deacons" (1985: 40).

Barnett states that "[i]n the light of the evidence from the Scripture and the early Church and of recent scholarship regarding the controversy and appointment of the Seven in Acts 6, we must conclude that the Seven were not deacons" (1995: 33).

Looking at the Scripture overall, there appears to be considerable room for interpretation of the purpose of the diaconate. It can be generally inferred that deacons principally held offices of supervision and that they provided some form of service which was administrative (as opposed to the ministry of the word associated with presbyters and episkopos) and which was noncultic in origin (Ziegler 1985). The role of deacons could be interpreted as the service well-pleasing to God (Hebrews 13) that all Christians are called to perform, but the deacons perform in an official and public way in the name of Christian community. The overall lack of specificity regarding deacons' functions might be considered a reflection of the early Church's culture when clearly defined institutions have not yet developed.

DEACONS' PURPOSE IN THE CHURCH TRADITION

Early Church (First to Fourth Century)

The period between the first, fourth, and sixth century, depending on the source (or from Ignatius of Antioch to Gregory the Great), is considered the Golden Age of the diaconate, because of the relatively high importance of deacons and their functions.

At the beginning of this period, the functions of the diaconate developed organically, with some differences between church communities in different geographic areas. This contributes to the ambiguity in our current understanding of those functions. Despite the contemporary critiques cited earlier in regard to tracing the diaconate to the Seven men appointed to the ministry of tables, the church leaders of this period began to rely on this reference in interpreting the role of diaconate (e.g., St. Irenaeus). Consequently, between the second and fifth century, the diaconate appears to have become a male-only order with women serving in the order of widows. The role of deacons in this period became increasingly defined although varied considerably between churches in different regions.

Based on the New Testament, and the *Didache* as well as the writings of Pope St. Clement I and Ignatius of Antioch, Echlin (1971) reconstructs the purpose of deacons in the first and second century as liturgy (including a possibility that deacons on occasion were authorized to preside over the Eucharist, but not authorized to conduct baptisms), charity (including assistance in administrating and distributing money, food and drink, serving the community, serving the bishop and obeying the clergy, as well as bearing letters between the churches), and word (including preaching, teaching, encouraging, reproving, correcting, and consoling).

The purpose of the diaconate between the second and fourth century can be derived from, among other sources, the writings of St. Polycarp and St. Hippolytus as well as from the *Didascalia Apostolorum*. According to St. Polycarp, the deacons' function was to symbolize Christ and, possibly, to serve along with bishops on the ruling council of some churches (Barnett 1995).

According to St. Hippolytus, the deacons' role was to serve the bishop, provide instruction during gatherings, bless non-Eucharistic bread in the bishop's absence, assist at baptisms, administer the Chalice and the Bread, as well as bring oblations from the faithful to the bishop (Barnett 1995).

According to the *Didascalia Apostolorum*, the deacons of the early Church were supposed to "hold the place of Christ" (or, "bear the likeness of Christ") and imitate Christ's example of service, enduring everything to the point of laying "down [their] life for [their] brethren in the ministry which is due to them." This ministry included "charity and brotherly love" to "sick and infirm," visiting "all who are in need" and informing "the bishop of those who are in distress," as well as serving as "the bishop's ear, mouth, heart and soul" (Connolly 2010). Deacons' duties also included guarding the door and keeping order during the Eucharist, as well as resolving disputes between the faithful. The number of appointed deacons was proportionate to the need of each local church. Perhaps, the most prominent example of this practice was Pope St. Fabian (third century) dividing Rome into seven zones and placing a deacon in charge of each for the promotion of charity and assistance to the poor.

While the current literature largely relies on the same primary sources, a few distinct interpretations might be worth noting. According to Searle, deacons' duties ranged: "from keeping order in the assembly to serving at table; to collecting the offerings; to selecting bread and wine for the Eucharistic meal; to helping distribute the Eucharistic bread and cup; to taking the Eucharist, together with gifts of food and clothing, to those whom age, infirmity, or imprisonment prevented from attending" (1985: 96).

Ziegler (1985) largely repeats the findings from Echlin (1971) but comes to different conclusions regarding the extent of deacons' cultic functions, observing that "that deacons assisted the bishop at the altar, and there are some scattered references to other cultic functions. It is clear, however, that the deacon was not ordained to the priesthood but to a ministry of various forms of service, usually performed in the person of the bishop" (Ziegler 1985: 10).

Barnett (1995) challenges a number of previous findings about the diaconate's purpose in the early Church. Most notably, he concludes that preaching was not among deacons' functions in that period. He notes that "in spite of the important place preaching had in the ministries of Stephen and Philip, and even though the Seven were thought by some to have been deacons from the time of Irenaeus, preaching was not part of the deacons' function as the office developed in the Church of the sub-apostolic age so far as is known, and it did not become so in the early Church" (33). Barnett (1995) also found evidence that deacons were allowed to baptize when commissioned by the bishop and that they took charge of small congregations.

Middle Ages (Fifth to Fifteenth Century)

Towards the end of the Golden Age of the diaconate, there are examples of deacons giving Eucharist to the presbyters and to non-presiding bishops in certain cities. There is some evidence that archdeacons held fiscal and judicial oversight over presbyters. The increasing power of deacons in some places and the ambiguity about the deacons' cultic role might have contributed to a growing tension between bishops and deacons on one side and presbyters on the other side, between the third and fourth century.

Those issues were examined and resolved at the Council of Nicaea (fourth century) when deacons were forbidden from offering Eucharist and became subservient to those who were allowed to offer it, the presbyters and bishops. The privileges of deacons were curtailed and the deaconesses were considered laity.[1] Beginning in the fourth and fifth centuries, the social role of deacon began to disappear. The purpose of the diaconate focused on liturgical support: announcing various stages of the Eucharist, reading the Gospel at the Eucharist, offering the prayers of the faithful at the Eucharist, announcing the kiss of peace, and blessing the paschal candle (Barnett 1995).

The Council of Toledo (seventh century) further curtailed the diaconate, reinforcing the subservient role of the deacon relative to that of a presbyter and referred to the deacon as a "servant" of bishops and presbyters. The importance of the diaconate continued to decline, although there are examples of deacons performing important services in the Church as late as the eleventh century.

During the Middle Ages, the diaconate survived only as a liturgical role mainly exercised by candidates preparing for priestly ordination. In this transitional form, the purpose of the diaconate became to enable "those who were to become priests to give proof of themselves, to display the merit of their work, and to acquire preparation—all of which were requirements for receiving the dignity of the priesthood and the office of pastor" (Pope Paul VI 1972). In this sense, the purpose of the transitional diaconate focused on training for presbyteral functions rather than on the practice of diakonia. A caveat should be added that late medieval legislation allowed for this transitional period to take several years (Echlin 1971).

Overall, the *diakonia* became increasingly a domain of religious communities "who assumed the responsibility of caring for the sick, feeding the poor, clothing and housing the impoverished, offering hospitality to travelers, and supporting widows and others who could not support themselves" (Searle 1985: 94–95). Perhaps, the most notable examples are St. Benedict (fifth–sixth century), St. Dominic (twelfth–thirteenth century), and St. Thomas Aquinas (thirteenth century). St. Francis (twelfth–thirteenth century) is particularly significant here for being both a religious friar and a deacon.

Notably, the religious congregations dedicated to *diakonia* did not completely substitute for the deacons, because they constituted "a class of ['specialists in diakonia'], who were either quite separate from or else very much peripheral to the life of the local Christian community of the parish" (Searle 1985: 95).

Modern Age (Sixteenth to Mid-twentieth Century)

During the counter-reformation, the Council of Trent (sixteenth century) explored the possibility of restoring the diaconate to its original function in the Church. One of the Council Fathers called for the restoration of the diaconate and its functions such as ministering at the altar, baptisms, mediating needs of the faithful to the bishop, as well as care of hospitals, widows, and those who are suffering (Echlin 1971). Much of the discussion at the council focused around the cultic role of deacons (i.e., whether deacons are supposed to minister at "sacred tables" or at "profane tables") and the ministry of the word (i.e., whether deacons should be allowed to preach).

While the council directed prelates to restore the functions of the diaconate, this directive was not implemented. The council concluded with diaconate remaining a temporary office. The functions of temporary deacons focused on ministry of word and liturgy. These functions included preaching, extraordinary ministry of baptism and Eucharist, as well as ordinary ministry of exposition. The ministry of charity was, in practice, limited to prayer and good example.

The subject of restoring a diaconate permanently exercised emerged in mid-nineteenth century Germany with the purpose of bringing the Church closer to the lay faithful (Hornef 1993 in Ditewig 2007). After World War II, interest in restoring a permanent diaconate was galvanized by the writing of two survivors of the Dachau concentration camp, Father Otto Pies and Father Wilhelm Schamoni. The scholarship of Father Karl Rahner further contributed to the topic. In 1951, a German social worker Hannes Kramer formed the first diaconate circle at the Social Workers Seminary in Freiburg (Olson 1992), which conducted research and advocacy for the cause of restoration. In 1959, after Pope St. John XXIII announced his intention to call a general council, Caritas International sent a petition for restoration of the diaconate to Council Fathers. The question of restoration was explored in 1963, with the United States opposing it. Ultimately, the council decided in favor of renewing the diaconate as a stable and permanent order of ministry on terms described in the next section.

DEACONS' PURPOSE IN THE
NORMATIVE DOCUMENTS OF THE CHURCH

The following subsection explores each of the functions in more detail by listing in a chronological order selected normative documents issued by the Holy See and the U.S. bishops from the Second Vatican Council onward.

Documents Issued in the 1960s

In 1964, Pope Paul VI promulgated the Second Vatican Council's *Dogmatic Constitution On the Church Lumen Gentium* which restored the institution of the diaconate. A caveat should be added that the diaconate was never formally abolished, and the constitution left establishing the diaconate to the discretion of the competent territorial bodies of bishops (subject to the approval of the Pope). According to the Constitution, the purpose of the diaconate is a participation in the Church's ministry of service (*diakonia*). More specifically, this service includes "the diaconate of the liturgy, of the word, and of charity to the people of God [which may include the duty to] administer baptism solemnly, to be custodian and dispenser of the Eucharist, to assist at and bless marriages in the name of the Church, to bring Viaticum to the dying, to read the Sacred Scripture to the faithful, to instruct and exhort the people, to preside over the worship and prayer of the faithful, to administer sacramentals, to officiate at funeral and burial services" (Second Vatican Council, *Lumen Gentium* 1964: §29).

In 1965, Pope Paul VI promulgated the Second Vatican Council's *Decree on the Missionary Activity of the Church Ad Gentes.* According to this decree, the purpose of instituting the diaconate is to do right by those men who *de facto* carry out work in the three areas of deacons' ministry identified in *Lumen Gentium*. The purpose of ordination to the diaconate is to strengthen them, improve their effectiveness, and bind them more closely to the altar. Therefore, the purpose of the diaconate can be found in the sacramental grace of the diaconate rather than in the functions reserved exclusively to the deacons.

In 1967, Pope Paul VI issued Motu Proprio an *Apostolic Letter Sacrum Diaconatus Ordinem: General Norms for Restoring Permanent Diaconate in the Latin Church* which established canonical norms for the renewed diaconate. According to the letter, the purpose of deacons (subject to authorization by the local Ordinary) is:

1. To assist the bishop and the priest during liturgical actions in all things which the rituals of the different orders assign to him;

2. To administer baptism solemnly and to supply the ceremonies, which may have been omitted when conferring it on children or adults;
3. To reserve the Eucharist and to distribute it to himself and to others, to bring it as a Viaticum to the dying and to impart to the people benediction with the Blessed Sacrament with the sacred ciborium;
4. In the absence of a priest, to assist at and to bless marriages in the name of the Church by delegation from the bishop or pastor, observing the rest of the requirements that are in the *Code of Canon Law*, with Canon 1098 remaining firm and where what is said in regard to the priest is also to be understood in regard to the deacon;
5. To administer sacramentals and to officiate at funeral and burial services;
6. To read the sacred books of Scripture to the faithful and to instruct and exhort the people;
7. To preside at the worship and prayers of the people when a priest is not present;
8. To direct the liturgy of the word, particularly in the absence of a priest;
9. To carry out, in the name of the hierarchy, the duties of charity and of administration, as well as works of social assistance;
10. To guide legitimately, in the name of the parish priest and of the bishop, remote Christian communities;
11. To promote and sustain the apostolic activities of laymen (Pope Paul VI 1967: §21).

In 1968, the U.S. Bishops' Conference submitted a request to the Holy See to establish the diaconate in the United States. The listed reasons include: completing the hierarchy of sacred orders, strengthening diaconal ministries with the sacramental grace of the diaconate, enlisting a new group of devout and competent men in the active ministry, extending needed liturgical and charitable services to the faithful, providing an official and sacramental presence of the Church in areas of secular life, as well as areas where few or no priests are available, and improving Church's ability to adapt to the rapidly changing needs of the society. The permission was granted the same year. The following year, the Bishops' Committee on the Permanent Diaconate was established. In 1969, the first permanent deacon was ordained in the United States. By 1971, thirteen diocesan diaconal programs were operating in the United States. The same year, the first cohorts of deacons were ordained in several dioceses (Ditewig 2006).

In 1968, Pope Paul VI promulgated the *Apostolic Constitution Pontificalis Romani Recognitio: New Rite Approved for Ordination of Deacons, Priests and Bishops* which contains approved official rites for diaconal ordination.

The document does not expand on the purpose of deacons beyond what was already stated in the *Lumen Gentium.*

Documents Issued in the 1970s

In 1971, the U.S. Bishops' Committee on the Permanent Diaconate published *Permanent Deacons in the United States: Guidelines on Their Formation and Ministry.* According to this document, the purpose of a deacon can be more properly defined in terms of who he is, rather than of what he does. The diaconal identity is based upon: "the invitation of the Spirit, the manifestation and realization of this call through sacramental ordination for the benefit of the universal Church, the special fraternal sharing of accountability for the kingdom with all ordained ministers, the acceptance by the community he is called to serve, and the complete personal commitment of self to serve in the name of Christ and His Church" (Bishops' Committee on the Diaconate 1971: §14). The guidelines state that the list of deacons' functions is wide, open-ended, and not exclusive of laity and priesthood. While deacons may perform a wide range of functions, these functions should be balanced between three ministerial areas of word, sacrament, and pastoral service. Finally, the guidelines give special attention to the needs for diaconal service in four communities: the black community, the Spanish-speaking community, the rural community, as well as on college and university campuses.

In 1972, Pope Paul VI issued Motu Proprio an *Apostolic Letter Ad pascendum: Norms for the Order of Diaconate* containing new norms for the diaconate that clarify, among other things, the rules for admission and for celebrating the Liturgy of the Hours. The letter does not directly explore the purpose of deacons beyond previously issued documents.

In 1974, Bishops' Committee on the Liturgy in the United States issued *Commentary on the Apostolic Letters of Pope Paul VI Ministeria Quaedam and Ad pascendum.* This commentary focuses in particular on the responsibilities of deacons concerning their prayer life—that deacons are supposed to pray in common either with their family or some community with which they are working pastorally.

In 1979, the Bishops' Committee on the Liturgy in the United States issued *The Deacon, Minister of Word and Sacrament.* According to this document, the purpose of deacons is "to serve the community in charity and justice. That ministry (. . .) is always related to the word and the altar" (39). As in the case of the commentary issued five years earlier, special attention is given to the role of deacons in community prayer (this time focusing specifically on the parish community).

Documents Issued in the 1980s

In 1983, Pope St. John Paul II promulgated the revised *Code of Canon Law*, which furnished more juridical material on the diaconate, such as the prerequisites for ordination (can. 1031–1037, 1039), and the process of formation (can. 236). Those revisions do not focus directly on furthering the understanding of the purpose of the diaconate.

In 1985, the U.S. Bishops' Committee on the Permanent Diaconate published *Permanent Deacons in the United States: Guidelines on their Formation and Ministry*. This publication was a revision to the 1971 document of the same title, prompted by the new formation guidelines in the *Code of Canon Law* and the desire to build on the accumulated contemporary experience with the diaconate (which did not exist at the time of the first publication). In comparison to the original guidelines, the purpose of the diaconate appears essentially the same. This document, however, further explains the purpose of the diaconate by focusing less on application into practice and more on integration into theology. The deacons' differentiating function is described as sacramental and as symbolic of the inner connection among the three great areas of the Church's life: word, sacrament, and service (i.e., "the ministry of love and justice"). The changes in the description of the deacons' purpose may be an indication of maturing institutional culture and the growth in collective understanding of the sacrament in the United States.

In 1985, Pope St. John Paul II gave a speech on the diaconate *Ai Partecipanti al Convegno dei Diaconi Permanenti: Allocution to Permanent Deacons* where he describes the purpose of diaconate on two levels. On a more personal level, the deacon is supposed to personify Christ, the servant of the Father, by participating in the threefold function (by proclaiming and illustrating the word of God, by administering the selected sacraments, by serving as a community animator, or by serving in ecclesial life). On a more organizational level, the purpose of the diaconate is to contribute to the birth of the Church as a reality of communion, service, and mission.

Documents Issued in the 1990s

In 1990, Pope St. John Paul II promulgated the *Codex Canonum Ecclesiarum Orientalium: Code of Canon Law for Eastern Rite Catholic Churches*, which builds on the 1983 Latin Code. It contains rules on the formation (can. 343) and ordination (can. 759–761) of deacons. It also governs the rights of deacons to carry out their ministry in the areas of preaching the word (can. 610) including giving homily (can. 614), participating in the celebration of the Divine Liturgy (can. 699, 1108) and administrating the sacraments (can. 677, 709).

In 1992, Pope St. John Paul II promulgated the *Catechism of the Catholic Church*. According to the Catechism, the purpose of deacons is to "serve the people of God in the diaconia of liturgy, word and charity, in communion with the bishop and his presbyterate" (§875, see also §1588). Deacons are the "ministers ordained for tasks of service of the Church (. . .) in the ministry of the word, divine worship, pastoral governance, and the service of charity, tasks which they must carry out under the pastoral authority of their bishop" (§1596).

In 1995, Pope St. John Paul II (1995) stated that the purpose of deacons is "to be a person open to all, ready to serve people, generous in promoting just social causes, avoiding attitudes or positions which could make him appear to show favoritism."

In 1998, the Holy See published two documents focusing on deacons with the intention to unify and clarify concepts, as well as to provide practical encouragement and more clearly defined pastoral objectives. The first document was prepared by the Congregation for Catholic Education and titled *Ratio Fundamentalis Institutionis Diaconorum Permanentium: Basic Norms for the Formation of Permanent Deacons*. This document states that the purpose of deacons is to exercise three gifts according to the specific perspective of diakonia: proclaiming the Scriptures, as well as instructing and exhorting the people, carrying out works of charity and assistance, and carrying out earlier defined sacramental functions. The three gifts are not equal in that "the diaconal ministry has its point of departure and arrival in the Eucharist, and cannot be reduced to simple social service" (§9).

The second document, published in 1998, was prepared by the Congregation for the Clergy and titled *Directorium Pro Ministerio et Vita Diaconorum Permanentium: Directory for the Ministry and Life of Permanent Deacons*. It describes the three areas of diaconal ministry in some detail; in particular, it explores the relationship of deacons to bishops, priests, and lack of priests. The connection between the three areas of diaconal ministry is explained in the following way: "the ministry of the word leads to ministry at the altar, which in turn prompts the transformation of life by the liturgy, resulting in charity" (Congregation for the Clergy 1998: §39). In describing the functions of deacons, the directory stresses the need for an ecumenical and collaborative attitude in deacons' ministry in the service of the community of the faithful.

Documents Issued in the 2000s

In 2004, the Congregation for Bishops issued the *Directory for the Pastoral Ministry of Bishops Apostolorum Successores*, an updated and revised version of the 1973 document intended to help bishops address the challenges and new problems of the present day in the Church and in the modern world. According to this document, the purpose of the diaconate is to proclaim and expound the word of God, to administer baptism, Communion and the sacramentals, and to animate the Christian community mainly in those areas relating to the exercise of charity and the administration of goods. Two caveats should be added about deacons' work in those ministries. First, deacons' work should be "pervaded by the *'sense of service'* (. . .) directed in the first place to God, and, in God's name, to the brethren" (§92). Second, while some of the tasks assigned to deacons "may also be performed by the lay faithful, they are always diaconal when performed by a deacon in the name of the Church, and sustained by the grace of the sacrament" (§92).

In 2005, the Bishop's Committee on the Permanent Diaconate promulgated the *National Directory for the Formation, Ministry, and Life of Permanent Deacons in the United States*. This document offers the most extensive treatment of the diaconate among all the normative documents listed here. It is intended to inform the process of preparing or updating diocesan diaconal formation programs and formulating policies for the ministry and life of deacons. The Directory reconstructs the purpose of deacons as evangelizers and teachers, sanctifiers, and as witnesses and guides. Two caveats should be made here. First, each deacon should be prepared to undertake each of the listed ministries. Second, deacons may engage in each of the listed ministries in diverse ways as determined by changing needs and individual predispositions.

Documents Issued in the 2010s

In 2012, Pope Benedict XVI issued Motu Proprio, an *Apostolic Letter Intima Ecclesiae Natura: On the Service of Charity*, which does not focus specifically on deacons, but instead explores the institutional vehicles for caring out charitable work by the faithful.

Notably, in the time period covered here, the Church issued a number of documents pertaining to an individual's suitability for ordination, including ordination to the diaconate. Those documents include, for example, *Circular Letters Concerning the Canonical Norms Relating to Irregularities and Impediments* (Congregation for Catholic Education 1992) or the *Instruction Concerning the Criteria for the Discernment of Vocations with Regard to Persons with Homosexual Tendencies in View of their Admission to the Seminary and to Holy Orders* (Congregation for Catholic Education 2005).

DEACONS' PURPOSE AND CONTEMPORARY UNDERSTANDING OF PHILANTHROPY IN THE UNITED STATES

To identify the place of deacons in the Church, this chapter to this point has depicted the purpose of the diaconate in terms of what it is and what it is not according to Church norms. Similarly, to identify the place of deacons in the American society at large, the purpose of diaconate may also be considered in the context of social norms pertaining to philanthropy.

Relationship Between Philanthropy and Diakonia

Philanthropy may be narrowly understood as giving of money by rich capitalists. As such it shares little with the diaconate. However, philanthropy can be also understood in a much broader context. The history of philanthropy can be traced to ancient Greece, where the term had several connotations, including (but not limited to) "theological" in reference to divine beings; ontological, in reference to an innate affection for human beings; social, in reference to the possession of certain social graces; or fiduciary, in reference to financial generosity (Sulek 2010b).

Similarly to the diaconate, the term "philanthropy" largely disappeared from European discourse and use during the Middle Ages. The term reemerged at the beginning of the fifteenth century and was increasingly used in several ways, including in reference to humanity (e.g., "love of God for humankind"); to describe activity focused on meeting a need and/or advancing human happiness; to describe human traits that impel people to want to help others; to describe an act of donating money, time, or effort; or to describe an organization that embodies an explicitly defined charitable cause (Sulek 2010a).

In contemporary American context, philanthropy can be understood as "voluntary action for the public good," where "voluntary" means unforced and free, where "action" refers to giving, serving, and associating, and where "public good" refers to services provided to others for whom one is not formally responsible (Payton and Moody 2008). According to Kraus (1997), there is a general tendency to perceive deacons as volunteers due to deacons often holding secular jobs and serving in their role "part-time." From this perspective, philanthropy may inform some aspects of deacons' service in American society and help refine the understanding of the diaconate in American culture. Notably, this does not mean that the diaconate can be exclusively described as a form of volunteering (Pope St. John Paul II 1985), or that it can be adequately defined as "charitable works" (Barnett 1995), because it cannot.

Egoistic Paradigm

Depending on the purpose it serves, philanthropy can be categorized into four general paradigms: egoistic (motivated by self-interest), compassionate (motivated by religious or humanitarian values and characterized by focus on more immediate needs), scientific (motivated by desire to systematically improve a particular human condition), and liberal (motivated by a desire for creating equality between the one serving and the one who is served) (Gunderman 2008). According to the egoistic paradigm, individuals engage in philanthropic activity for the purpose of personal gain. While this may appear not Christian-like, it should be noted that egoistic does not mean misanthropic. From the point of view of psychological egoism, every human action is motivated by self-interest, and from the point of view of ethical egoism, human behavior should promote self-interest.

The purpose of the diaconate can be framed, in the egoistic paradigm, as, for example, the accrual of after-life benefits (Thornton and Helms 2010). Regardless of self-interested motivation, egoistic philanthropy may be perceived as overall beneficial to society, if one believes that philanthropy is never "bad" (Kelley 2008) or that philanthropy always serves some understanding of public interest (Kristol 2008).

Compassionate Paradigm

The compassionate paradigm can be described as a model of philanthropy historically aiming to satisfy immediate human needs. In America, formal expression of this model can be traced to John Winthrop's "Model of Christian Charity," written in 1630 (Cheek, Kramarek, and Rooney 2015). Compassionate philanthropy is rooted in religious tradition in all three Abrahamic faiths: in Judaism compassionate philanthropy can be traced to the concepts of *tikkun olam* (repairing the world) and *tzedekah* (works of charity, justice); in Christianity, it finds expression in the concepts of *caritas* (unlimited loving kindness to all others), *tithing* (donating a fraction of one's income), and *diakonia* (service); in Islam, it relates to concepts of *takaful* (social solidarity), *zakat* (donating a fraction of one's wealth), *waqf* (endowments), and *sadaqa* (benevolence) (Ilchman, Katz, and Queen 1998). Framing the work of deacons operating within predominantly Christian American society in the context of other religious belief systems may allow for better understanding of the norms regarding charity specific to the Catholic tradition.

In addition to encompassing religious charity, the compassionate paradigm also includes compassionate humanitarianism. The difference between religious charity and compassionate humanitarianism can be exemplified in the lives of Mother Theresa and Princess Diana (Orwin 2002)—both canonized as saints of compassion (one by the Catholic Church, the other one by public opinion). The core difference between them can be found in the stance each took with respect to suffering. For Princess Diana, suffering was "the main enemy and its eradication the final goal" (Orwin 2002: 96). For Mother Theresa, suffering was recognized as "necessary to the salvation of sinful human beings" (Orwin 2002: 96). For the former, charity was a merely human virtue with a merely human point of reference—the relief of human suffering. For the later, suffering was redemptive and charity was a manifestation of human aspiration for the divine and transcendental.

Another difference between religious charity and compassionate humanitarianism can be found in the scope of each approach. Relative to compassionate humanitarianism, Christian service is not compartmentalized, but rather encompasses faith, hope, and charity, as well as a unity of action and contemplation. In "this theology the word 'service' does not denote service to others; rather it refers to service of the Gospel through worship, word, and work" (Hypher 1985: 40).

In the context of those distinctions, deacons may struggle to understand and to being understood by their secular counterparts in the process of providing service to others, because from the standpoint of Catholic charity, compassionate humanitarianism may seem shallow and superficial, while from the standpoint of compassionate humanitarianism, Catholic charity may appear self-interested and ineffective. Understanding and appreciating those distinctions may be particularly relevant in places such as hospital chaplaincy or prison chaplaincy, where deacons may carry out their ministry alongside social workers and chaplains representing other religions (with each group following differently defined norms under one umbrella of philanthropic activity).

In addition to the differences between various philanthropic workers, it is important also to point out the main similarity between them, which is a desire to volunteer one's time to act altruistically on higher values even if those values are not the same. Past research tends to indicate that higher motivation to act on one's values is positively associated with volunteering. For example, Anderson and Moore (1978) found that concern for others predicts one's propensity to volunteer. Sokolowski (1996) found that the strength of one's altruistic orientation had an effect on the amount of volunteering. Frisch and Gerrard (1981) found that volunteers were motivated primarily by altruism. Toppe, Kirsch, and Michel (2001) found that 96 percent of all volunteers (and 98 percent of volunteers to religious organizations) considered compassion towards others to be an important reason for volunteering. Kramarek (2016) found that a motivation for acting or expressing important convictions concerning serving others was a statistically significant predictor of the frequency of volunteering, and that this motivation was the most important of the six functional motivations identified in the study.

Scientific Paradigm

The third paradigm of philanthropy can be referred to as a scientific paradigm, as it aspires to use systematic, rational, and efficient ways of improving selected aspects of the human condition, often based on objective, measurable indicators (Smith, Stebbins, and Dover 2006). In American, technology-focused society, scientific philanthropy finds particular appeal. This does not always appear justified, however. In some fields (e.g., medical treatment), scientific philanthropy is highly successful. In other fields, its effectiveness is not as clear (Cheek, Kramarek, and Rooney 2015).

Deacons may benefit greatly from adopting a scientific paradigm in certain areas of their ministerial activity: for instance, when applying for funding, when trying to communicate with secular authorities in language the mainstream population will understand, and when seeking to increase the tangible outcomes of their work, etc. (Hoge 1994).

Liberal Paradigm

The fourth paradigm of philanthropy is called liberal philanthropy (Gunderman 2008). It has a few distinguishing characteristics: it is created on the foundation of the golden rule; it identifies the goal of philanthropy as helping people "to develop larger, more complete conceptions of themselves as human beings, and to help them progress further along those paths" (Gunderman 2008: 33); thus it extends the subject of philanthropy from the materialistic to the spiritual in a post-modern way; and by calling for a holistic approach to human need, it demands holistic involvement (i.e., philanthropy should be present in every sphere of one's life, including work); it provides the means of accomplishing the goal of philanthropy by the concept of sharing forward—thus transforming "receivers into givers" (Gunderman 2008: 24) and creating equality between the one serving and the one who is served. This paradigm is exemplified in the activities of Dorothy Day and Peter Maurin's Catholic Worker Movement, Muhammad Yunus' Garmeen Bank in Bangladesh or Jane Addams' Hull House in Chicago, IL.

Deacons may benefit from exploring this paradigm as they are balancing the competing priorities of their family life, work life, and obligations to the Church. This paradigm also allows one to reframe philanthropy not only as a service but also as an act of communion and an act of establishing the strongest bonds of friendship. As such it might be exemplified in the washing of the feet before the Last Supper (Campbell 2006).

CONCLUSION

A description of the diaconate can be presented in two distinctively different ways, depending on whether the focus is on the norms or on the actual behavior of deacons. This chapter focused on the first, normative, approach by attempting to reconstruct the purpose of the diaconate based on the scripture, Church tradition, normative documents of the Church, and contemporary norms guiding philanthropy in American society in general. The remainder of this book is based on the second, descriptive, approach. This descriptive approach acknowledges that there is a gap between the teachings and actual practice of religion, and focuses on the latter, describing what is, rather than what should be.

NOTE

1. There are different possible explanations for the decisions to diminishing the role of diaconate. For example, according to Brown, those reasons might have included: "the stress on church unity in the face of factions that developed, the influence of the Roman preoccupation with order, the need for strong leadership at the time of persecution, and an awareness of uniqueness within the Church as the new Israel and the centrality of Eucharist in its life" (Brown in Ziegler 1985: 4).

According to Searle, the institution of religious freedoms and later adoption of Christianity by Constantine the Great in the fourth century led to the increase in the number of the faithful. This, in turn, led to the increasing need and importance of the presbyters and to the institutionalization of the Church. The common Eucharistic meal shared at a table by a small community in a private house was replaced by a public observing a "Eucharistic ceremony" performed by a select few. In the process, Christian faithful were transformed from "participants in a common sacred meal" to "spectators at a sacred drama performed by the men with the power." In the context of those developments, the "connection between the sacred liturgy and works of charity and justice carried out in the world became quite attenuated" (Searle 1985: 99). Furthermore, the increasing sacralization of the liturgy led to the increasing perception that liturgy is the opportunity to encounter the Divine. By contrast, works of service carried outside of liturgy lacked this quality. This relatively decreased the role of diakonia and, consequently, of the deacons.

Chapter Two

How is the Diaconate Changing?

Trends in the Presence and Ministry of Deacons

Mary L. Gautier

This year marks the fiftieth anniversary (1968–2018) of the restoration of the diaconate as a stable and permanent order of ministry in the United States. Chapter 1 presented a normative history of the diaconate, exploring how the role was understood in the early Church, based on Scripture and Church Tradition, and how it gradually devolved into a minor liturgical role for men preparing for ordination to priesthood. The chapter also outlined the history of its restoration, culminating with Pope Paul VI issuing Motu Proprio, his *Apostolic Letter Sacrum Diaconatus Ordinem: General Norms for Restoring the Permanent Diaconate in the Latin Church* in 1967. A year later, on August 30, 1968, Pope Paul VI granted the petition of the U.S. bishops for the restoration of the diaconate in the United States.

We also noted in chapter 1 how the understanding of the diaconate has evolved over time as the Church grows more familiar with this restored order. From the original canonical norms for the diaconate, which were codified by Pope Paul VI in *Sacrum Diaconatus Ordinem*, lived experience with deacons working alongside priests and bishops has led to a deeper and more profound understanding of what deacons do and their role in the hierarchy of clergy. In this chapter, we explore trends in the growth and expansion of the diaconate around the world and in the United States over the last fifty years. For the United States, we also explore some of the evolution in understanding about what it is that deacons do in their ministry, informed by three major national studies on the diaconate in the United States as well as other CARA research on the diaconate.

EMERGENCE OF THE DIACONATE AROUND THE WORLD

The permanent diaconate was not restored all at once around the world. The United States was among several countries, mostly in Europe, who were among the early adopters. And today, most of those countries with the oldest diaconate programs—Germany, France, Italy, and Brazil—are among those with the largest presence of deacons (Ditewig 2006: 33). In fact, 40 percent of all deacons in the world serve in the United States. According to Vatican statistics, the United States has 18,033 diocesan deacons (*Annuarium Statisticum Ecclesiae* 2015). Europe has 14,206, with the majority in Italy (4,372), Germany (2,992), and France (2,672). The only other countries reporting more than a thousand deacons in 2015 are Brazil (4,080), Canada (1,276), and Chile (1,136).

As Table 2.1 shows, the diaconate worldwide grew most rapidly in the first decade after its restoration, increasing from just over 300 deacons in 1970 to more than 7,000 just ten years later. The population more than doubled again between 1980 and 1990, exceeding 17,000 worldwide. The world total number of deacons more than doubled again between 1990 and 2010. In the last five years, between 2010 and 2015, the world population of deacons has increased by 14 percent to nearly 45,000. Overall, the number of deacons increased faster in the earlier decades (an additional 7,055 deacons worldwide during the 1970s compared to an increase of 11,699 deacons during the 2000s) while the rate of growth slowed down (from 2,283 percent in 1970s to 43 percent in 2000s).

The number of deacons relative to the overall size of the Catholic population in a region illustrates another interesting trend in the data. Because deacons typically come from within the Catholic population of an area, one would expect that areas with large Catholic populations would also have larger numbers of deacons. This is not the case in all countries, however. For example, while the United States, Great Britain, Germany and Austria—with populations well in excess of 5 million Catholics—each have more than

Table 2.1. Growth of the diaconate by world region, 1970–2015.

World Region	1970	1980	1990	2000	2010	2015
Africa	16	119	254	345	378	397
Americas	111	5,782	12,414	18,157	25,235	29,379
Asia	12	33	52	87	190	254
Europe	166	1,382	4,311	8,540	12,857	14,206
Oceania	4	48	89	176	344	391
Grand Total	309	7,364	17,120	27,305	39,004	44,627

Source: *Annuarium Statisticum Ecclesiae*, respective years.

Table 2.2. Deacons per million Catholics by world region, 1970–2015.

World Region	1970	1980	1990	2000	2010	2015
Africa	0.4	2.0	2.9	2.7	2.0	1.8
Americas	0.4	15.0	26.9	35.0	43.1	47.0
Asia	0.2	0.5	0.6	0.8	1.5	1.8
Europe	0.6	5.1	15.1	30.5	42.8	49.7
Oceania	0.9	8.3	12.7	21.5	34.9	38.3

100 deacons per million Catholics, so does Puerto Rico, with a Catholic population of a little more than 3 million (*ASE* 2012). In fact, the Bahamas, Sweden, Jamaica, and the U.S. Virgin Islands each have more deacons per million Catholics than the United States. And while Italy has about 71 deacons per million Catholics in a country of more than 58 million Catholics, Switzerland, Iraq, and New Zealand have nearly the same ratio although they have far smaller Catholic populations (3.5 million, 0.3 million, and 0.6 million, respectively). Those countries have many more deacons than would be expected, given their much smaller Catholic population.

Table 2.2 displays the growth in the diaconate across world regions as the ratio of deacons per million Catholics in a region. One can see here that the ratio was most stark in Asia in 1970. With just 12 deacons in a population of approximately 50 million Catholics, the ratio was 0.2 deacons per million Catholics. Africa and the Americas had roughly similar ratios—about 0.4 deacons per million Catholics, and the situation in Europe and in Oceania was just slightly more favorable, with 0.6 and 0.9 deacons per million Catholics.

Over time, however, the ratio of deacons per million Catholics improved dramatically, especially in the Americas, in Europe, and in Oceania. By 2015, each of those world regions had roughly 40 to 50 deacons per million Catholics.

The ratio in Africa and in Asia, in contrast, has improved much more slowly, reaching 1.8 deacons per million Catholics in 2015. In Asia, which had the least favorable ratio in 1970, the increase has been steady each decade since that time. In Africa, the ratio of deacons per million Catholics improved until 1990, but has declined since then, as the growth in the Catholic population has outpaced growth in the diaconate. Perhaps in decades to come the ratio of Catholics to deacons will catch up in those world regions as well.

EMERGENCE OF THE DIACONATE IN THE UNITED STATES

CARA has been following the development of this ministry in the United States almost since the very beginning. CARA has also been tracking the development of diaconate formation programs in the United States and the

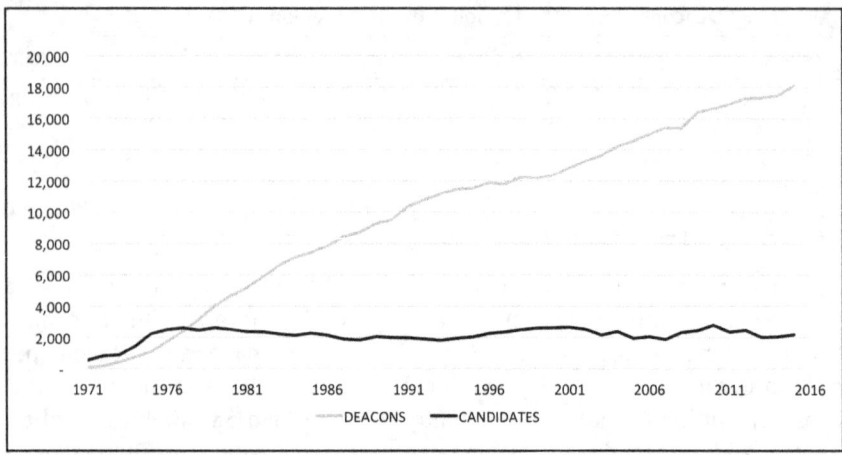

Figure 2.1. Number of deacons and deacon candidates.
Sources: CARA *Catholic Ministry Formation Directory; The Official Catholic Directory*.

men being formed in those programs, collecting annual data on formation programs and deacon candidates since 1996.

The number of deacons in the United States has grown steadily since its restoration in 1968. Figure 2.1 displays the steady growth of this ministry from 58 deacons in 1971 to 18,045 in 2016 (an average increase of 45 deacons a year), with another 2,500 in formation. Deacons presently serve in every state in the United States and the District of Columbia. They serve in every diocese and archdiocese and in most of the eparchies of the Eastern Churches.

Looking closer at the growth trend in the diaconate within the United States, we see similar patterns of rapid growth in the early years as dioceses worked to establish formation programs and identify suitable candidates. Thirteen formation programs were initially approved by the U.S. Bishops for preparing deacons: the Archdioceses of Baltimore, Chicago, Detroit, Hartford, and San Antonio each had a program, as well as the Dioceses of Galveston-Houston, Des Moines, Gallup, Phoenix, and San Diego. In addition, three other programs were established by the Josephite Fathers (for the Archdiocese of Washington and the Diocese of Richmond), Ss. Cyril and Methodius Seminary in Orchard Lake, Michigan, and St. John's University in Collegeville, Minnesota (Bishops' Committee on the Diaconate 1971: 3). These original programs prepared approximately 430 candidates, of which a total cohort of 58 were ordained in 1971 (Bishops' Committee on the Diaconate 1985: 2).

From just a few dozen candidates in a handful of dioceses that established formation programs in the 1970s, by 1980 a total of 124 U.S. dioceses reported 4,093 deacons in ministry. The largest numbers of deacons were reported by the Archdioceses of Chicago (400 permanent deacons), Newark (200), Galveston-Houston (105), Hartford (137), New York (116), and the Dioceses of Dallas (101).

The total number of deacons in the United States grew from a little over 4,500 in 1980 to nearly 10,000 in 1990. Ten years later, in 2000, the total number of deacons in the United States had grown to more than 12,000. By 2010, they numbered close to 17,000, and by 2015, they totaled more than 18,000, an increase of some 350 percent over those thirty-five years.

Table 2.3 displays the archdioceses and dioceses that reported more than 200 deacons in 2015. Most of those who reported more than 100 deacons in 1980 are still on the list, and they have been joined by many other archdioceses and dioceses who are also experiencing rapid increases in the diaconate. Some of the interesting patterns that can be seen in these trends include:

- The Archdiocese of Chicago was among the original thirteen to establish a formation program for the diaconate and has had two administratively separate formation programs for English-speaking and Spanish-speaking deacons. Chicago had the largest number of deacons of any U.S. diocese in 1980, and is still the archdiocese with the largest total number of deacons.
- The Archdioceses of Galveston-Houston and Los Angeles each reported about 100 deacons in 1980, but have grown since then to more than 400 deacons each, making them the second- and third-largest in terms of the total number of deacons, after Chicago.
- The Archdioceses of Philadelphia and Atlanta, as well as the Diocese of Austin, each had fewer than ten deacons in 1980. They grew rapidly and by 2000 Atlanta had 137 deacons, while Philadelphia and Austin each had more than 180. By 2015, each of them had well over 200 deacons and Philadelphia had nearly 300.
- The Archdioceses of Newark and Hartford, which were among the largest in 1980 with 200 and 137 deacons, respectively, have increased more slowly than other dioceses and each has reported declines in recent decades as their older deacons retire and die.

Another way to measure the presence of the diaconate in a diocese is to compare the total number of its deacons to the total size of its Catholic population (as reported by dioceses in *The Official Catholic Directory* 2017). By that measure, several dioceses who have a smaller Catholic population have a more favorable ratio of deacons per thousand Catholics. Adjusting for the size of the Catholic population in a diocese, the Dioceses of Fairbanks and Lexington have the most favorable ratio, with about two deacons for every thousand Catholics. Fairbanks has 2.42 deacons per thousand Catholics and

Table 2.3. Growth of the diaconate in the United States, 1980–2015.

Archdiocese/Diocese	1980	1990	2000	2010	2015	Deacons per Thousand Catholics in 2016
Archdiocese of Chicago	400	568	618	656	652	.29
Archdiocese of Galveston-Houston	105	220	296	378	438	.24
Archdiocese of Los Angeles	91	214	188	314	407	.11
Archdiocese of New York	116	293	343	373	388	.15
Diocese of Trenton	91	183	268	380	368	.40
Archdiocese of San Antonio	77	203	284	356	360	.50
Archdiocese of St. Louis	29	142	225	268	301	.53
Archdiocese of Philadelphia	1	101	188	247	294	.21
Diocese of Rockville Centre	50	167	219	273	292	.19
Archdiocese of Boston	92	180	190	247	284	.14
Archdiocese of Washington	92	183	226	198	276	.41
Archdiocese of Atlanta	6	110	137	242	247	.24
Archdiocese of Omaha	63	118	142	249	239	1.00
Archdiocese of New Orleans	40	149	192	211	237	.45
Diocese of Phoenix	62	121	207	239	233	.20
Diocese of Brooklyn	54	139	152	178	222	.15
Archdiocese of Detroit	93	156	146	187	221	.20
Diocese of Cleveland	23	116	174	215	216	.32
Archdiocese of Santa Fe	45	98	146	216	215	.64
Diocese of Austin	5	61	181	207	210	.39
Archdiocese of Hartford	137	266	308	280	209	.38
Diocese of Joliet in Illinois	36	145	152	198	208	.37
Archdiocese of Cincinnati	57	114	137	201	207	.50
Diocese of Paterson	69	89	158	209	203	.46
Grand Total in all U.S. Dioceses	4,711	9,340	12,837	16,840	18,105	.27

Source: *The Official Catholic Directory*, respective years.

Lexington has 1.85. Six eparchies of the Eastern Churches have a similar favorable ratio. Another thirteen dioceses have at least one deacon for every thousand Catholics in the diocese. These include:

- Archdiocese of Omaha (1 deacon per thousand Catholics)
- Diocese of Peoria (1.03 deacons per thousand Catholics)
- Diocese of Knoxville (1.06 per thousand)
- Diocese of Superior (1.08 per thousand)
- Diocese of Amarillo (1.11 per thousand)
- Diocese of Memphis (1.12 per thousand)
- Diocese of Jefferson City (1.13 per thousand)
- Diocese of Nashville (1.14 per thousand)
- Diocese of Rapid City (1.16 per thousand)
- Diocese of Duluth (1.17 per thousand)
- Diocese of Tulsa (1.18 per thousand)
- Diocese of Bismarck (1.20 per thousand)
- Personal Ordinariate of the Chair of St. Peter (1.73 per thousand)

TRENDS IN ACTIVE AND RETIRED DEACONS

In the United States, deacons may not be ordained until they are at least thirty-five years of age, married or celibate (Bishops' Committee on the Diaconate 2005: 40). Many enter the diaconate after they have retired from a secular career. Thus, deacons tend to be a little older than Catholics in general. Nevertheless, deacons overall tend to serve many years in active ministry. Many deacons continue to serve in a more limited capacity well into their seventies and eighties, long past their "retirement" from active ministry. More than half of dioceses have a mandatory retirement policy for deacons in active ministry: about eight in ten dioceses require deacons to retire at age 75; another tenth of dioceses set age 70 as a mandatory retirement age for deacons.

The very large numbers of deacons that were ordained in the 1970s, 1980s, and 1990s have by now mostly retired from active ministry, but they have largely been replaced by the men who entered after them. Thus, as can be seen in Figure 2.2, the proportion of all living deacons nationally who are still active in ministry has declined by only ten percentage points in the last twenty years—from 88 percent active in 1996 to 78 percent active in 2016.

Almost eight in ten deacons nationally are currently active in ministry. Of those who are no longer in active ministry, about 80 percent are "retired," although, as mentioned above, a sizable minority continues to serve in a

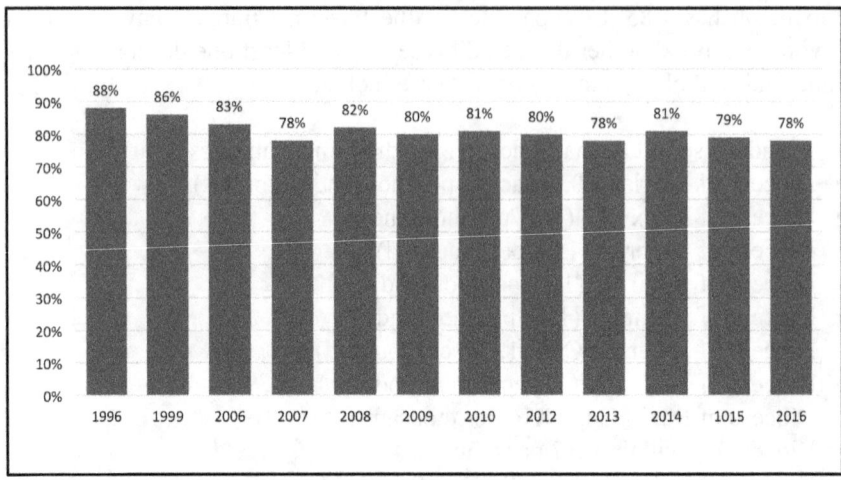

Figure 2.2. Percentage of deacons nationally in active ministry.
Sources: NCCB Triennial Survey of the Diaconate, 1996 and 1999; CARA Diaconate Post-Ordination Reports, 2006–2016.

more limited capacity. The remainder is on a leave of absence, inactive for some other reason, or suspended from active ministry. As expected, the largest archdioceses and those with the longest history of deacons—Chicago, Galveston-Houston, Los Angeles, and Hartford—also have the largest numbers of deacons who are retired or no longer in active ministry.

TRENDS IN THE MINISTRY STATUS AND COMPENSATION OF ACTIVE DEACONS

Deacons are ordained to "extend the liturgical and charitable services of the bishop" (Bishops' Committee on the Diaconate 1985: 1) and their service extends far beyond the liturgical role in parish life in which they are most commonly observed. According to the 1971 Guidelines:

> The deacon, therefore, is more properly defined in terms of who he is rather than of what he does. He is a person with a special mission requiring special relationships within the community of God's people. With such a self-understanding, the deacon will realize that his roles, his duties, his functions of service are to be performed not only in response to the needs of the people but also in the light of all those relationships by which his office of deacon is verified. His functions will not be limited by historical precedent but will show a flexibility and a creativity that express his identity in any given place and milieu where the Holy Spirit invites his ministry. However much these functions may vary, the essential elements of diaconal identity remain: the

invitation of the Spirit, the manifestation and realization of this call through sacramental ordination for the benefit of the universal Church, the special fraternal sharing of accountability for the kingdom with all ordained ministers, the acceptance by the community he is called to serve, and the complete personal commitment of self to serve in the name of Christ and his Church (Bishops' Committee on the Diaconate 1971: §14).

As was noted in chapter 1, the various documents of the Church have described seven purposes (or functions) of the diaconate: to complement the orders of priests and bishops, to symbolize Christ the Servant, to serve God and the people of God, to exercise sacramental grace, to strengthen the ministry of deacons, to increase the Church's organizational capacity to address diverse needs, and to perform the prescribed functions of the deacon in liturgy, sacraments, and sacramentals, as listed in the normative documents of the Church. These functions have evolved over time as our understanding and experience of deacons in the Church and in the world have unfolded.

Just like other ordained clergy, deacons who dedicate themselves to ecclesiastical ministry should be compensated for their ministry. Unlike bishops and priests, however, the Church recognizes that deacons typically are engaged in or retired from secular employment, which provides for their material needs. Canon 281 §3 states: "Married deacons who devote themselves completely to ecclesiastical ministry deserve remuneration by which they are able to provide for the support of themselves and their families. Those who receive remuneration by reason of a civil profession which they exercise or have exercised, however, are to take care of the needs of themselves and their families from the income derived from it." The U.S. Bishops also state that: "Permanent deacons are to take care of their own and their family's needs using income derived from their full-time employment by the diocese, parish, or secular profession" (Bishops' Committee on the Diaconate 2005: §94). Thus, although nearly all are married, their ministry as a deacon is largely uncompensated. Some deacons are employed in a secular (non-ministry) position in addition to their diaconal ministry. A smaller number of deacons are employed in a compensated Church ministry, in addition to their diaconal ministry, which we explore in more detail in the next section. Whether working in a career or retired, however, deacons serve in a myriad of ways in active ministry.

To gain some perspective on the ways that deacons today are engaged in active ministry, we first examine findings from a national poll of permanent deacons conducted by CARA in 2001 (Gray and Gautier 2004). Looking at the responses of deacons surveyed more than fifteen years ago and then comparing them to the responses of the deacons we surveyed in 2017 will illuminate some trends in diaconal ministry, which we will explore in more detail in chapter 5.

In 2001, about four in ten responding deacons (38 percent) indicated that they were employed in a secular job in addition to their ministry as deacons. Younger deacons, as expected, were more likely than older deacons to say they held a secular job in addition to their ministry as deacons. Half of the deacons (45 percent) surveyed in 2001 were working forty hours or more at their secular job while still serving as a deacon. Today, the proportion of deacons working in a secular job is about the same (43 percent) as it was in 2001. About six in ten (57 percent) are retired from secular employment or not currently working. Just as in 2001, half of the deacons with secular employment say they work at least forty hours a week at their secular job in addition to their diaconal ministry.

Nearly all deacons are assigned to a parish for at least a portion of their ministry. In the 2001 poll, more than a third of deacons reported parish ministry as their only ministry, while six in ten said they were engaged in both parish and non-parish ministry (such as a chaplaincy position in a hospital or a prison). Just 2 percent indicated that their ministry was entirely non-parish—even deacons assigned to a full-time diocesan position, such as a diocesan director of the Office of Permanent Deacons, typically assist the pastor in their local parish on the weekends. Today, the proportion of deacons who are currently engaged in both parish and non-parish ministry is slightly higher than it was in 2001—about two-thirds of deacons in the 2017 survey are engaged in both parish and non-parish ministry. Three in ten are engaged in parish ministry only, compared to 36 percent in 2001, and just 4 percent say their ministry is entirely non-parish ministry.

Compensated Ministry

In addition to their uncompensated diaconal ministry, about one in three active deacons in 2017 (35 percent) is also employed in a compensated ministry position, either as a part-time or a full-time employee. The proportion of deacons also employed in a compensated ministry has not changed much over time. In surveys that CARA has conducted since 2006, Diocesan Diaconate Directors consistently estimate that a fifth to a third of their deacons are also employed in a compensated ministry. Most commonly, deacons may be employed in a parish ministry position, such as a Director of Religious Education, Director of Liturgy, or Youth Minister. Slightly fewer, on average about 14 percent of active deacons in a compensated ministry, are employed in a non-ministerial capacity in a parish, typically in positions involving administration, business, or finance.

Deacons also serve in hospital ministry (15 percent of all deacons serving in a compensated ministry); in prison ministry (12 percent); in a diocesan ministerial position, such as a Director of the Office of Deacons (8 percent); in a diocesan non-ministerial position, such as administration or finance (9 percent); in parochial education, such as a teacher or a principal (5 percent); or in social services, such as Catholic Charities (3 percent). These percentages are compiled from the estimates provided by Diocesan Diaconate Directors; the actual work that deacons do in their ministry is explored in more detail in chapter 5.

An interesting trend in compensated ministry for deacons involves deacons who are entrusted with the pastoral care of a parish that has no resident priest pastor: a "can. 517 §2 parish" (in reference to the *Code of Canon Law*). Some 13 percent of active deacons in a compensated ministry are in such a position. This position involves both pastoral care and administrative responsibilities, and a number of bishops see deacons as uniquely suited for this responsibility. The position was codified in the 1983 *Code of Canon Law*, which outlines the conditions under which a bishop may entrust a parish to a deacon, a religious sister or brother, or another lay person, in canon 517 §2:

> If the diocesan bishop should decide that due to a dearth of priests a participation in the exercise of the pastoral care of a parish is to be entrusted to a deacon or some other person who is not a priest or to a community of persons, he is to appoint some priest endowed with the powers and facilities of a pastor to supervise the pastoral care.

CARA has studied the application of can. 517 §2 parishes across the United States and documented the trend in several publications (see Gray, Perl, and Gautier 2008). Figure 2.3 shows how the number of parishes entrusted to someone other than a priest increased through the beginning of the twenty-

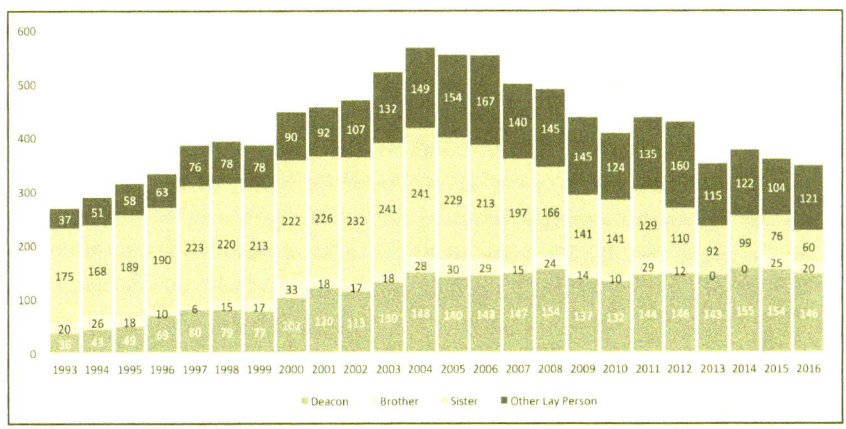

Figure 2.3. Parishes entrusted to someone other than a priest.
Source: The Official Catholic Directory.

first century, as bishops struggled to keep up with a mismatch between the numbers of parishes and the number of priests available to staff them.

The other clear trend that can be seen in Figure 2.3 is the increasing number of deacons called into this ministry. Lay persons were also employed in increasing numbers for this position, as the numbers of women religious available for such service has declined. But the overall trend line shows that the total number of can. 517 §2 parishes peaked in 2004, and has been decreasing since then as bishops find other ways to deal with a shortage of priests. Although the decline in the overall number of can. 517 §2 parishes has continued, the number of deacons entrusted with these parishes remains virtually unchanged since 2004. As of the beginning of 2017, according to *The Official Catholic Directory*, a total of 146 can. 517 §2 parishes are entrusted to deacons.

TRENDS IN DIACONATE FORMATION AND THREE ORDINATION COHORTS

As the numbers of deacons have increased, and as the ministries in which they are engaged have broadened and deepened, formation for the diaconate has also developed over time to meet changing realities. Diaconate formation is described in more detail in chapter 4. The U.S. Bishops' Committee on the Permanent Diaconate issued a document entitled *Permanent Deacons in the United States: Guidelines on Their Formation and Ministry*, published in 1971, which guided the formation of the earliest cohorts of deacon candidates. This document was necessarily quite broad and open, drawn largely from a report of the Catholic Theological Society of America on the theology of the diaconate as well as the very early experience of the first diaconate programs (Bishops' Committee on the Diaconate 1985: 2).

After several years of lived experience with deacons and their formation, the Bishops' Committee on the Permanent Diaconate commissioned a comprehensive study of the diaconate in the United States, published in 1981 as *A National Study of the Permanent Diaconate in the United States*. The Bishops' Committee incorporated the findings from that study and the wisdom gained from more than a decade of experience in diocesan formation programs across the country into a revision of the guidelines, which were republished under the same title in 1985.

In 1993, the Bishops' Committee on the Permanent Diaconate again commissioned a major national study of the diaconate in the United States. This study was published in 1996 as *A National Study on the Permanent Diaconate of the Catholic Church in the United States: 1994–1995*. Informed by the findings from that study as well as extensive work by the Vatican's Congregation for Catholic Education and the Congregation for the Clergy, who promulgated the *Basic Norms for the Formation of Permanent Deacons* and the *Directory on the Life and Ministry of Permanent Deacons* in 1998, the U.S. Bishops issued a third revision of the guidelines, published in 2005 as the *National Directory for the Formation, Life and Ministry of Permanent Deacons in the United States*. This document guides formation of deacon candidates today and there is a fourth revision of the guidelines currently underway.

Recognizing that the formation of deacons likely evolved as each of these three sets of guidelines were implemented across diocesan formation programs, we use the publication date of these documents to construct three cohorts of deacons. The first cohort consists of those deacons prepared for ministry under the influence of the first set of guidelines, the men who were ordained between 1971 and 1985. The second cohort includes deacons ordained between 1986 and 2005, who were formed under the influence of the revised guidelines. The third cohort includes deacons ordained between 2006 and 2017, whose formation took place under the third revision of the guidelines. In later chapters, where applicable, we compare the responses of deacons from each of these cohorts to see how their attitudes about diaconal ministry and the ministries in which they are engaged may vary according to the guidelines that formed them for ministry.

Trends in Diaconate Formation Programs

As mentioned at the beginning of this chapter, CARA has been following diaconate formation programs for the last twenty years, reporting the statistics on these programs and the men in formation each year. Active diaconate formation programs currently exist in all fifty states and in the District of Columbia. Active programs are found in 167 of the 195 U.S. dioceses and eparchies. Table 2.4 displays the growth in these formation programs over this 20-year span.

Although the data in Table 2.4 do not allow for any comparison between Cohort 1 (ordained 1971 through 1985) and Cohort 2 (ordained 1986 through 2005) in their formation experience, it does display some interesting trends between Cohort 2 and Cohort 3 (ordained 2006 or later), designated by the horizontal line between 2004–2005 and 2005–2006. Notice that the number of candidates was substantially greater in 2004–2005 than the number in 2005–2006, as some bishops briefly suspended their diaconate formation programs so that they could be reorganized in light of the new guidelines. Note also that the number of reporting formation programs held steady at about 135 programs until after the new guidelines were released, when the number

Table 2.4. Diaconate formation program enrollments, 1996–2017.

Year	Aspirants*	Candidates	Average Enrollment	Reporting Programs	Anticipated Ordinations
1996–1997		2,247	22	102	149
1997–1998		2,238	22	104	36
1998–1999		2,370	22	109	209
1999–2000		2,497	20	125	552
2000–2001		2,606	21	125	124
2001–2002		2,575	20	126	273
2002–2003	897	2,470	18	135	558
2003–2004	1,240	2,144	16	136	470
2004–2005	958	2,342	17	135	580
2005–2006	1,134	1,903	14	133	444
2006–2007	1,042	2,105	15	141	547
2007–2008	1,067	1,963	14	139	560
2008–2009	1,433	2,319	14	167	582
2009–2010	1,457	2,445	15	168	498
2010–2011	945	2,775	17	172	578
2011–2012	982	2,302	18	158	722
2012–2013	1,098	2,468	16	172	801
2013–2014	1,291	2,018	18	167	521
2014–2015	1,104	2,051	17	166	420
2015–2016	1,082	2,297	17	165	569
2016–2017	1,002	2,670	16	168	523

*CARA first asked programs to report aspirants in 2002–2003.

Source: *CARA Catholic Ministry Formation Directory, 2017.*

of programs began to increase again. Finally, it is interesting to note that the number of anticipated ordinations to the diaconate peaked in 2004–2005 at 580 ordinations, just as the new guidelines were being published. The number of candidates, programs, and ordinations all increased steadily after the new guidelines were released.

Among the 168 active diaconate formation programs in 2017, half were established in the 1970s. Just 5 percent of the active programs today were established before 1970. About a quarter of active programs were established in the 1980s or 1990s and a fifth have been established since 2000 (Gautier and Holland 2017: 23). The characteristics of contemporary diaconate formation programs and the candidates in formation are described in more detail in chapter 4.

CONCLUSION

The restoration of the diaconate as a stable and permanent order of ministry has been widely accepted in the United States; perhaps more so here than in any other country in the world. From its very beginning fifty years ago, U.S. bishops have organized formation programs and large numbers of men have responded to the call and served enthusiastically. As bishops gained experience in working with deacons, they gradually revised the guidelines for their formation and ministry. This chapter traced some of the trends in the implementation of the diaconate in the United States, showing how the diaconate spread across the dioceses and how the ministries of deacons expanded as experience with the restored order increased. Finally, the chapter documented some of the trends in the implementation of diaconate formation programs and showed how the revision of guidelines for their formation and ministry affected those formation programs.

The next chapter will explore the characteristics of deacons in the United States, using historical data from CARA's archive as well as a new comprehensive national survey of deacons in the United States.

Chapter Three

Who are the Deacons?

Demographic Characteristics of Deacons

Mary L. Gautier

The 3,166 deacons responding to the 2017 survey of the diaconate come from all fifty states and the District of Columbia. They hail from 191 dioceses and archdioceses, including five deacons that were ordained abroad but now reside in the United States. An additional seven responding deacons were ordained for three U.S. eparchies and one responding deacon was ordained as a member of a religious order.

Nine in ten responding deacons (90 percent) are currently active. Another 6 percent are not active, but still assist at Mass or serve as a deacon in some way. Notably, deacons in active ministry are a little more likely than all deacons in general to respond to the questionnaire, but the characteristics of these responding deacons fairly represent the characteristic of all permanent deacons in the United States (Gautier and Holland 2017). This chapter explores the characteristics of these responding deacons, to better understand who deacons are.

AGE, GENERATION, AND ORDINATION COHORT

In the United States, deacons must have attained age thirty-five to be ordained (Bishops' Committee on the Diaconate 2005: 87). The youngest deacon to respond to the survey was 37 and the oldest was 98. The average age of responding deacons is 68. Most deacons are in their sixties (40 percent) or their seventies (32 percent), but about a fifth are in their fifties or younger. Thus, the average age of deacons is roughly equivalent to the average age of priests in the United States, which was 63 in 2009, when CARA last conducted a national survey of priests (Gautier, et al. 2012: 3).

It is also useful to compare deacons according to their generation, since those who came of age during different time periods typically shared cultural experiences that have shaped their attitudes and behaviors. For church research, we compare Catholics according to these generational categories:

- Deacons of the Pre-Vatican II generation were born prior to 1943 and came of age well before the Second Vatican Council. They are 75 years or older in 2017 and make up nearly a quarter of all deacons responding to the survey (23 percent). These deacons, for the most part, grew up in working class, ethnic Catholic neighborhoods where they were immersed in a supportive and nurturing Catholic culture. Their experience in growing up Catholic included the Baltimore Catechism, the Latin Mass, and parishes staffed almost entirely by priests. If they attended Catholic schools, they were taught mostly by Catholic sisters and religious brothers. Institutional loyalty is a key value for members of this generation, among Catholics as well as those of other faith traditions.
- Vatican II deacons were born between 1943 and 1960 and are between the ages of 57 and 74 in 2017. About two-thirds of all deacons in this study (67 percent) are members of the Vatican II generation. On average, Catholics of this generation grew up in a more suburban and more affluent environment than the generation before them, as the children and grandchildren of immigrant Catholics who had gradually assimilated into American society and moved into the middle class. These deacons largely came of age during and immediately following the Second Vatican Council, a time of great turbulence and rapid change, in the Church and in American society in general. They lived through the implementation of the reforms of Vatican II while they were growing up, with the change to Mass in English instead of Latin, the flattening of the hierarchy as Catholics accepted the notion of Church as the People of God, and the empowerment of lay people to be formed and trained for lay ecclesial ministry. They also witnessed the restoration of the diaconate as an ordained ministry open to married men.
- Post-Vatican II deacons were born between 1961 and 1981 and are between the ages of 36 and 56 in 2017. A tenth of the deacons in the study (10 percent) are in this generation. Catholics of this generation have come of age after the Second Vatican Council. For them, the Council is a historical fact, not something they personally experienced. Immersed in American culture rather than the ethnic Catholic subculture of their grandparents, they have had to seek out their Catholic identity in parish life, Catholic schools, and Catholic organizations. They have never known a time when the Mass was not said in English or when lay people were not active in parish ministry. These deacons are also the first generation to have experienced deacons

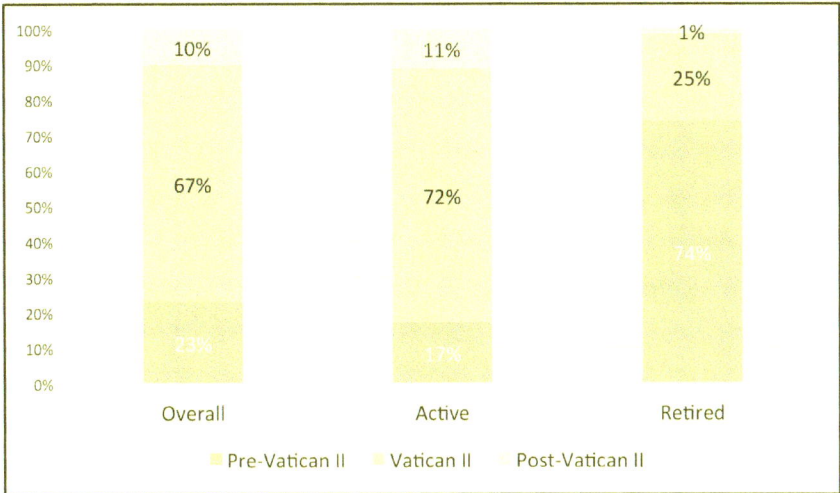

Figure 3.1. Active and retired deacons by generation.
Graphic courtesy of the author.

ministering in the parishes where they grew up, so they have always had this as a ministry alternative.

As shown in Figure 3.1, deacons involved in active diaconal ministry are predominantly of the Vatican II and Post-Vatican II generations, although an impressive 17 percent of active deacons are of the Pre-Vatican II generation. Among the retired deacons, as expected, about three-quarters are of the Pre-Vatican II generation and a quarter are Vatican II generation. The very few Post-Vatican II deacons who are not currently in active ministry still serve as deacons and told us in their comments on the deacon survey (e.g., moved to a new diocese, new work responsibilities, family circumstances) why they are not in active ministry at this time.

Finally, it is useful for us to compare deacons according to their ordination cohort. This term derives from the particular USCCB formation document that guided the formation of deacons. See chapter 1 for a description of the three formation documents within the greater development of the diaconate after the Second Vatican Council, and chapter 2 for a description of how CARA operationalized these three cohorts. Figure 3.2 displays the generational distribution of each ordination cohort.

Those deacons who were formed and ordained under the first set of guidelines for the diaconate are now 79 years of age or older and are mostly retired. Three in four are of the Pre-Vatican II generation and about a quarter are Vatican II generation. Deacons that were formed and ordained under the second

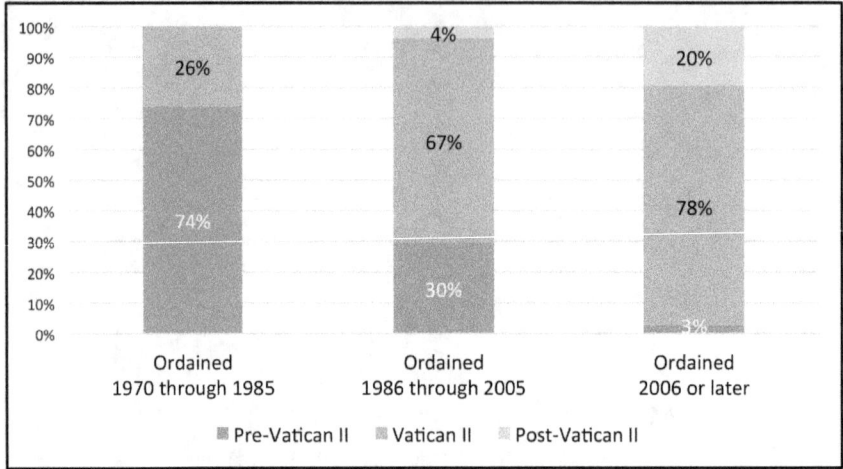

Figure 3.2. Ordination cohorts by generation.
Graphic courtesy of the author.

set of guidelines (ordained 1986–2005) average 70 years of age. About two in three of that cohort are Vatican II generation and three in ten are Pre-Vatican II generation. A very small proportion (4 percent) of that ordination cohort are Post-Vatican II generation—men who were in their mid- to late-thirties when they were ordained in the very early years of the twenty-first century. The deacons who were formed and ordained under the third set of guidelines (ordained in 2006 or later) average 62 years of age now and are mostly Vatican II generation (78 percent) or Post-Vatican II generation (20 percent). Just a few (3 percent) are Pre-Vatican II generation deacons—men who came to the diaconate at a more advanced age.

RACE AND ETHNICITY

Just as the U.S. Catholic population is becoming more racially and ethnically diverse (Zech, et al. 2017:14), so too are deacons. We can see this increasing diversity when we compare deacons engaged in active diaconal ministry to those who are now retired from active ministry (Figure 3.3). Although the majority of deacons (almost nine in ten) are white, an increasing proportion are Hispanic or Latino (7 percent among active deacons, compared to just 4 percent among retired deacons).

This increasing diversity among deacons is proving to be an invaluable asset for priests in parish ministry, particularly in parishes that are rapidly growing in the South and West. One in seven deacons is fluent in a language other than English, and more than one in ten report that they sometimes preach in

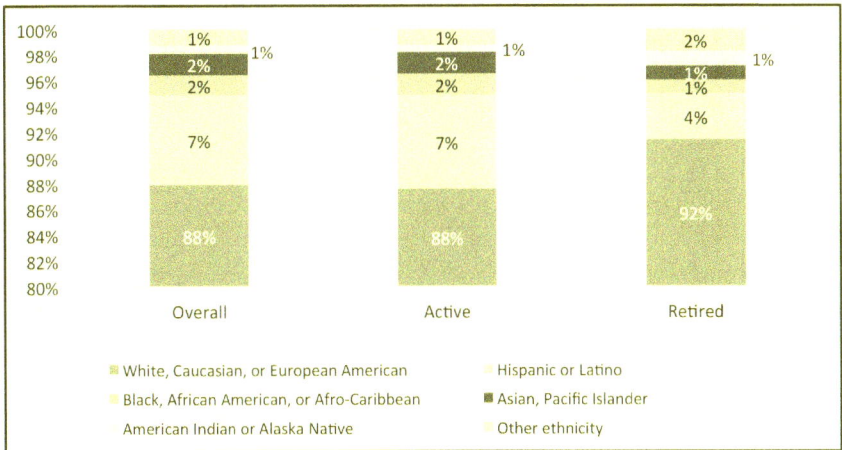

Figure 3.3. Active and retired deacons by race/ethnicity.
Graphic courtesy of the author.

a language other than English. This is especially helpful for pastors who may not be fluent in any language other than English. They can rely on their multi-lingual deacon for ministry to the ethnic and cultural sub-groups of the parish, particularly if the deacon shares their culture and language.

Some of the deacons shared their thoughts with us, in their open-ended comments at the end of the deacon's survey, about the ways that they often serve as a bridge across cultures:

As a deacon, I baptized over 12,700 children and preached off and on at Spanish services at my parish.

Deacons should be able to learn and communicate in Spanish, especially in performing liturgies (i.e., homilies, funeral rites, communion services).

I work in a parish with only two fluent speakers in Spanish, myself (age 71) and the Parochial Vicar (age 29). The most frustrating, never-ending part of my job as Director of Latino Ministries is explaining time and again to the Anglos why Latinos act/react as they do, and vice-versa. Yet still I encounter skepticism and ignorance more often than not. I have a M.A. in Latin American Studies, have worked 30 years in various Latin countries, yet I don't feel believed by Anglos when I explain the Latinos.

. . . the multi-cultural dimensions that our Church is experiencing and how we adapt our programs and services [to those realities], not merely translating from English to Spanish.

I like to bridge the diversity of different cultures, languages, and ethnic backgrounds: the acceptance of people regarding their beliefs and practices to different forms of celebrating in their own cultural practices.

Planning and implementation to include church members from all cultures. For example, have priests who can communicate and work effectively in attracting people from different ethnicities. The goal would be not to just have an all-black, all-Hispanic, all-Anglo, all-oriental, etc. congregation, but to have a balance.

RELIGIOUS FORMATION AND CATHOLIC SCHOOLING

Most deacons were Catholic from birth, either Latin rite (84 percent) or Eastern rite (1 percent). Some 15 percent of deacons converted to Catholicism at a later point in their life, on average at age thirty.

In terms of their faith formation, about two in three deacons (64 percent) attended a parish religious education program while they were growing up. About four in ten (39 percent) attended a parish or diocesan youth ministry program while they were in their teens and one in six (16 percent) attended a Catholic campus ministry program. Table 3.1 shows that deacons are more likely than other Catholic males ages 35 and older to have participated in each of these faith formation programs while growing up.

Table 3.1. Participation in religious formation while growing up.

Religious Formation Program/Activity	Deacons %	Catholic Males Ages 35 and Older* %
Parish religious education program	64	44
Parish/diocesan youth ministry	39	8
Catholic campus ministry	16	3
One or more years of post-college volunteer service	5	—

*Data on Catholic males ages 35 and older are from CARA Religion and Science Poll, May 2016.

For some deacons, their vocation is an outgrowth of a longer history of commitment to volunteer service in the Church. One in twenty (5 percent) participated in a year or more of post-college volunteer service, like the Jesuit Volunteer Corps or the Vincentian Volunteers.

Catholic Schooling

Deacons are also more likely than other Catholic males of similar ages to have attended Catholic schools for at least some of their education (Table 3.2).

Close to two in three deacons attended Catholic schools for their elementary education and nearly half attended a Catholic high school. In general, Catholic males ages 35 and older are roughly half as likely as deacons to have attended Catholic schools for their elementary and high school education.

Table 3.2. Attendance in Catholic schools.

Level of Catholic Schools Attended	Deacons %	Catholics Males Ages 35 and Older* %
Catholic elementary or middle school	63	42
Catholic high school	48	20
Catholic college or university (undergraduate)	32	8
Catholic college or university (graduate school)	25	

*Data on Catholic males ages 35 and older are from CARA Religion and Science Poll, May 2016. For this group, the question asking about attendance at a Catholic college or university did not distinguish between undergraduate and graduate school attendance.

Deacons are also significantly more likely than other Catholic males of comparable age to have attended a Catholic college or university. A third of deacons attended a Catholic college at the undergraduate level and a quarter attended one at a graduate level, compared to less than 10 percent of Catholic males in the general population who had that experience at either the undergraduate or graduate level.

Among all deacons, members of the Pre-Vatican II generation are more likely than the later generations to have attended a Catholic high school or to have attended a Catholic college as an undergraduate (see Figure 3.4). However, they were significantly less likely than later generations of deacons to have participated in Catholic campus ministry.

Comparing deacons according to their ordination cohort, we notice that each cohort is equally likely to have attended a Catholic elementary or middle school (approximately two in three of each cohort) or a Catholic high school

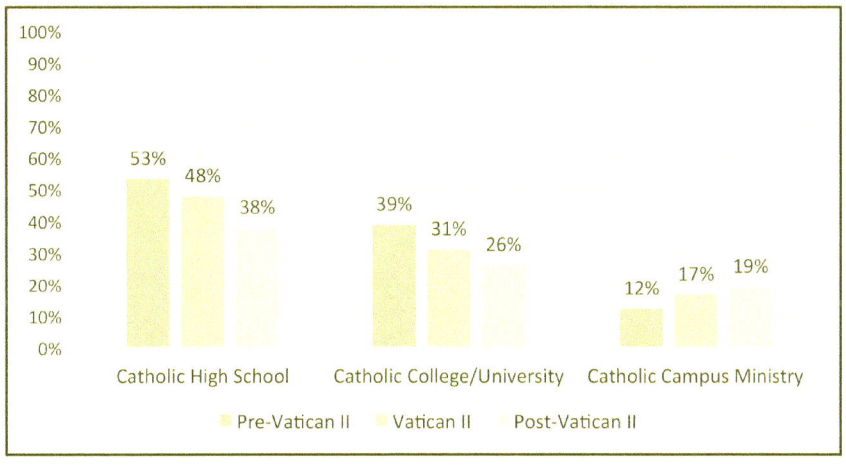

Figure 3.4. Catholic schooling by generation.
Graphic courtesy of the author.

(approximately 44 to 54 percent), but earlier cohorts are more likely than later cohorts to have attended a Catholic college for their undergraduate education: 44 percent of those ordained in 1970 through 1985, compared to 35 percent of those ordained in 1986 through 2005, and 27 percent of those ordained in 2006 or later. The same pattern holds for those who attended Catholic college for their graduate studies, although the differences are not as sharp.

Consideration of a Vocation to Priesthood or Religious Life

Deacons are also more likely than a comparable group of never-married Catholic men to have considered, or even pursued, a vocation to priesthood or religious life. According to a poll CARA conducted in 2012 of never-married Catholic men, a quarter of Pre-Vatican II, 15 percent of Vatican II, and 7 percent of Post-Vatican II Catholic men, have considered a religious vocation at least "a little" seriously (Gray and Gautier 2012). While the questions are not strictly comparable, the deacons in our 2017 deacon survey were asked if they ever considered becoming a priest or a religious brother, Figure 3.5 shows that about six in ten deacons of each generation considered a vocation to priesthood or religious life at least "a little" seriously, a much higher percentage than among never-married Catholic males.

In fact, 15 percent of these deacons have "very seriously" considered becoming a priest or a religious brother, and 17 percent say they were enrolled in a seminary or in formation for a religious order at some time in their past. On average, these deacons had entered the seminary (or novitiate, in the case

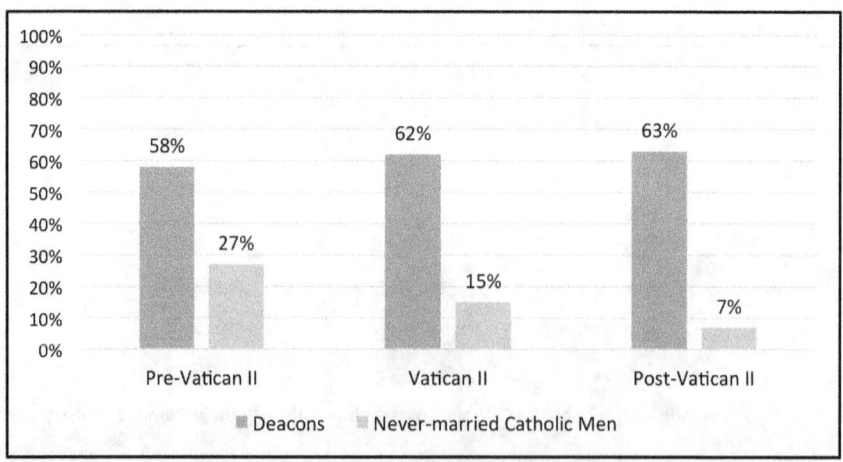

Figure 3.5. Considered a vocation to priesthood or religious life at least "a little" seriously.
Graphic courtesy of the author.

of a religious order) at age 17 and had left, on average, at age 21. While this was a not-uncommon pattern among young Catholic men of the Pre-Vatican II and Vatican II generations, it is striking to note that the same pattern occurred among these Post-Vatican II generation deacons: close to two-thirds considered a vocation at least "a little seriously" and 12 percent actually enrolled in a seminary, on average at age 19.

Men of each ordination cohort do not differ from each other in the proportion who has "very seriously" considered becoming a priest or a religious brother (between 14 and 19 percent), but they do differ from one another in whether they were ever enrolled in a seminary or in formation for a religious order: a quarter of deacons in the earliest ordination cohort (ordained 1970 through 1985) had been enrolled in a seminary, compared to 19 percent of those in the 1986 through 2005 ordination cohort and 13 percent of those in the latest cohort (ordained in 2006 or later).

SECULAR EDUCATION AND EMPLOYMENT

Compared to other Catholic males ages 35 and older, deacons are very well-educated. A third (32 percent) of Catholic men ages 35 and older have attained at least a bachelor's degree or more, but close to half (47 percent) have a high school degree or less. In contrast, just 5 percent of deacons have no more than a high school degree and three in four (76 percent) have a bachelor's degree or higher.

Among the 76 percent of college-educated deacons are 24 percent with a bachelor's degree, 33 percent with a graduate degree in a field not related to the diaconate, and 19 percent with a graduate degree in theology, religious studies, canon law, or some other field related to the diaconate. Chapter 5 will describe in detail the ministries in which deacons are engaged and chapter 2 dealt with deacons' compensated ministries, so this section will focus specifically on the secular employment of deacons.

Besides their work as a deacon, about a third of permanent deacons (34 percent) are employed full-time in a secular job. Another 10 percent are employed part-time in a secular job. Just over half (53 percent) of responding deacons say that they are currently retired from a secular job, and just 4 percent say that they are not currently employed. As expected, younger deacons are much more likely than older deacons to be full-time employees (Figure 3.6). Among deacons employed in secular jobs, full-time workers average 45 hours per week in their job and part-time workers average 20 hours per week.

We did not ask deacons to tell us the type of secular jobs they hold, but many deacons have very practical skills from their secular employment

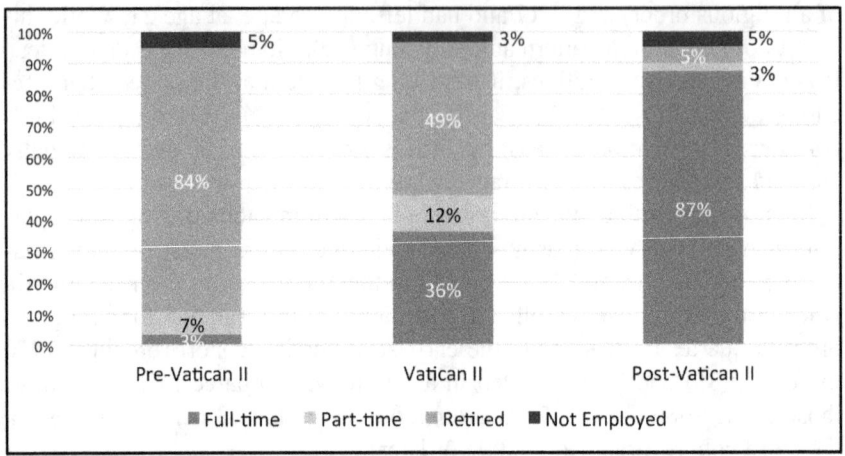

Figure 3.6. Secular employment by generation.
Graphic courtesy of the author.

that they bring with them to their diaconal ministry. One bishop told us in a focus group:

> . . . we have a number of permanent deacons, especially in the cities, who are business administrators in the parishes and because of that I will just assign them that parish also for their diaconal ministry. But they are excellent administrators. They are much more interested in it than a lot of the pastors are and take the burden off the pastors.

Other deacons bring skills in finance, human resources management, engineering, and many other areas that are often an invaluable asset to their ministry.

MARITAL STATUS AND PRESENCE OF CHILDREN IN THE HOUSEHOLD

More than nine in ten deacons are currently married (93 percent). Another 5 percent are either separated or divorced (1 percent) or widowed (4 percent). Just 2 percent are single, never-married. Among the married deacons, nearly all are married to another Catholic (98 percent).

As shown in Figure 3.7, Pre-Vatican II deacons (12 percent) are more likely than younger generations to be widowed, while Vatican II and Post-Vatican II deacons are more likely than older deacons to be married. A nearly equal percentage among each generation is single, never married: 1 percent of Pre-Vatican II deacons and 2 percent of Vatican II and Post-Vatican II deacons. Chapter 7 takes up the topic of deacons' wives in great detail, and

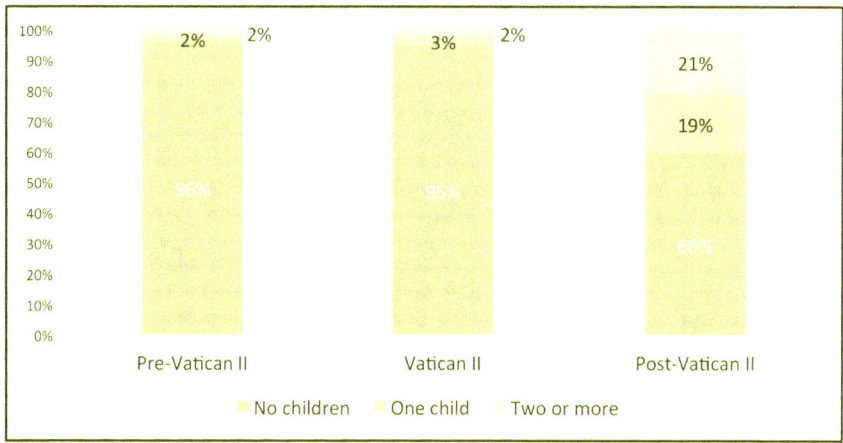

Figure 3.7. **Marital status by generation.**
Graphic courtesy of the author.

describes how diaconal ministry affects these families and how these families, in turn, affect parish ministry.

Most deacons (91 percent) have no children or stepchildren under age 18 currently living in their home. Younger deacons are more likely to have children living at home, but 5 percent of Pre-Vatican II and Vatican II deacons have one or more children living at home (Figure 3.8). Among Post-Vatican II deacons, on average they have one child or stepchild still living in the home.

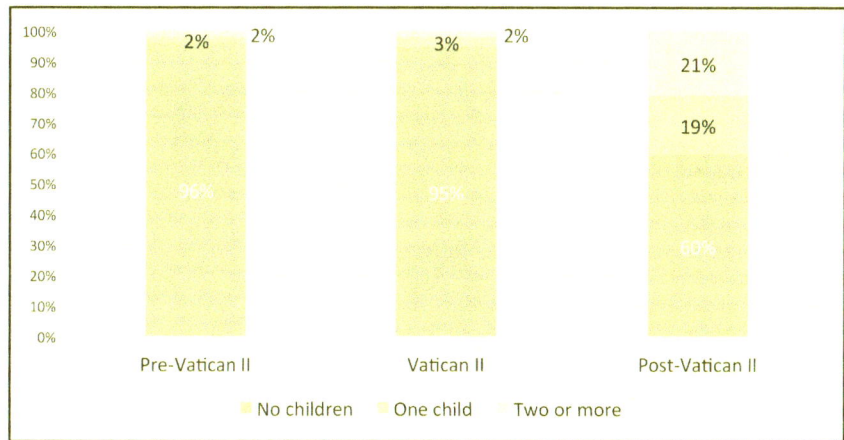

Figure 3.8. **Children/stepchildren living at home by generation.**
Graphic courtesy of the author.

PLACE OF RESIDENCE

We asked deacons to tell us the arch/diocese in which they currently live as well as their arch/diocese of ordination. Among those who responded to those questions, the biggest share of responding deacons (33 percent) currently live in the South (USCCB Regions IV, V, X, and XIV), followed by 29 percent who live in the Midwest (USCCB Regions VI, VII, VIII, and IX). Almost one in four responding deacons (23 percent) live in the Northeast (USCCB Regions I, II, and III) and about a seventh (14 percent) live in the West (USCCB Regions XI, XII, and XIII). Figure 3.9 offers a more nuanced view by displaying the percentage distribution of responding deacons by the state where they currently live.

Some deacons moved from the arch/diocese in which they were ordained. Overall, some 13 percent of responding deacons were ordained in a different diocese from the one where they currently reside. A few deacons in this group reported considerable differences in diaconal experience between the dioceses where they served. For example, one deacon described his experience as follows:

> *I was much more inspired, supported, and utilized in the Archdiocese where I was ordained. I feel much less understood, utilized, and appreciated . . . where I am now. My sense is that the people here neither understand deacons, nor the larger diaconate.*

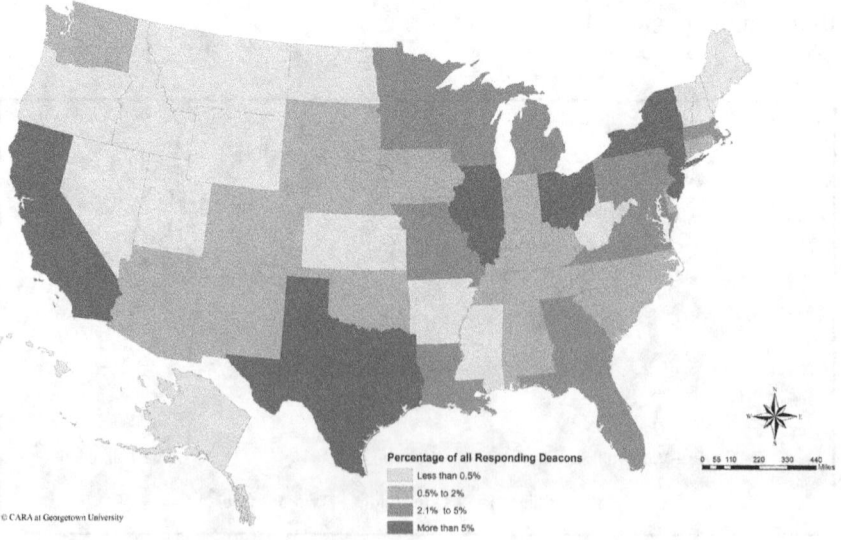

Figure 3.9. Responding deacons by state.
Graphic courtesy of the author.

Age by Residence

Deacons in the Northeast tend to be a year or two older than those in other regions of the country (see Table 3.3). The average age of responding deacons in the Northeast is 69 among all deacons and 68 among the active deacons. Active deacons in the Midwest and in the South tend to be a year or two younger than those in other regions, with an average age of 66 among active deacons in those two regions, compared to 67 among responding active deacons in the West and 68 among responding active deacons in the Northeast.

Table 3.3. Age of responding deacons by their current residence.

	All Responding Deacons			Active Deacons		
	Mean	Median	Range	Mean	Median	Range
Midwest	67	68	37–95	66	66	37–90
Northeast	69	69	41–95	68	68	41–94
South	67	67	37–96	66	66	37–91
West	68	69	39–98	67	68	39–85
All Deacons	*68*	*68*	*37–98*	*67*	*67*	*37–94*

DIACONAL HISTORY

Deacons overall were in their mid-forties, on average, when they first considered the diaconate, in their late forties when they were accepted into candidacy for the diaconate, and in their early fifties when they were ordained. Those responding to the deacon survey have served, on average, more than fifteen years as a deacon. About 1 percent has served less than a year, having been ordained in 2017, and just over 2 percent have served more than forty years as a deacon.

Interestingly, when we compare the deacons by ordination cohort we see that earlier cohorts of deacons were younger than later cohorts when they first considered the diaconate, were accepted as candidates, and were ordained, on average (Table 3.4).

Table 3.4. Average age of deacon milestones by ordination cohort.

	Ordained 1970–1985	Ordained 1986–2005	Ordained 2006 or Later
First seriously considered becoming a deacon	37	43	47
Accepted as a candidate for the diaconate	38	47	52
Ordained as a permanent deacon	41	51	57

Table 3.5. Average age of deacon milestones by generation.

	Pre-Vatican II	Vatican II	Post-Vatican II
First seriously considered becoming a deacon	46	45	37
Accepted as a candidate for the diaconate	49	49	42
Ordained as a permanent deacon	53	53	46

Comparing by generation, as we have done in the earlier parts of this chapter, shows something quite different (Table 3.5). Pre-Vatican II and Vatican II deacons were about the same age, on average, when they first seriously considered becoming a deacon, when they were accepted as a candidate, and when they were ordained. Post-Vatican II deacons, in contrast, are about seven to ten years younger than the older generations when they reached each of these deacon milestones. This difference, and its consequences, is explored in more detail in chapter 4.

CONCLUSION

Deacons in the United States are a diverse group. They include men of various ethnic and racial backgrounds. They have different levels of education, including their Catholic education. Their marital status and family situations are different. They are in different places in their secular work lives. Yet all of them share in the call to diaconate. In the next chapter we explore how this diverse group of men navigates their lives in an effort to pursue this call. In other words, what does it take for those men to be deacons?

Chapter Four

What Does It Take to Become a Deacon?

Deacons' Vocation and Formation

Michal J. Kramarek

This chapter provides a description of what it takes to be a deacon, mainly based on the guidelines included in the current *National Directory for the Formation, Ministry, and Life of Permanent Deacons in the United States* (from here on referred to simply as *Formation Directory*) prepared by the Bishops' Committee on the Diaconate (2005) as well as data from several nationwide empirical studies. Unless indicated otherwise, the findings presented here derive from the most recent of those studies—CARA's 2017 national survey of 3,166 active and retired deacons ordained between 1970 and 2017.[1]

The question of what it takes to become a deacon is explored here by investigating deacons' paths through different phases of their lives, including initial discernment, pre-ordination, and post-ordination. Particular attention is given to the help deacons received on this journey in the form of formation programs. The second part of this chapter is devoted to deacons' assessment of those programs and suggestions for improvements.

THE LIFE CYCLE OF DEACONS

Deacons' paths through different phases of their lives related to pre-discernment, discernment, formation, and ministry is illustrated in Table 4.1, which provides an overview of those phases for all deacons in the United States ordained between 1970 and 2017. The first three phases are applicable to some, but not all, deacons: enrollment in seminary or formation for religious order, departure from those programs, and conversion to Catholicism. The phases that virtually all deacons go through include the first consideration of the diaconate, acceptance into candidacy and start of the formation process, the ordination, and, eventually, retirement from active ministry as a deacon.

Table 4.1. Age (in years) at different stages of deacon's life (all responding deacons).

	Mean	Median	Range
Enrolled in seminary or in formation for a religious order*	17	16	10–45
Left seminary or formation for a religious order*	21	20	13–44
Converted to Catholicism	30	28	4–64
First seriously considered becoming a deacon	44	45	13–69
Accepted as a candidate for the diaconate	48	49	24–72
Age when began formation	48	49	27–73
Ordained as a permanent deacon	52	53	31–77
Current age	68	68	37–98
Fully retired (or expect to fully retire) from diaconal ministry	76	75	51–100

*if applicable

Notably, those ordained under different national formation guidelines for permanent deacons in the United States complete those phases at different time in their lives. As described in more detail in chapters 1 and 2, the national formation guidelines were first published in 1971, and later revised in 1984 and again in 2005. As Figure 4.1 shows, the deacons formed after each of these publications (ordination cohorts) differ notably from each other.

Deacons ordained in the oldest cohort (1970 through 1985) first considered the diaconate, on average, six years earlier than deacons ordained in the middle cohort (1986 through 2005), and 11 years earlier than those ordained

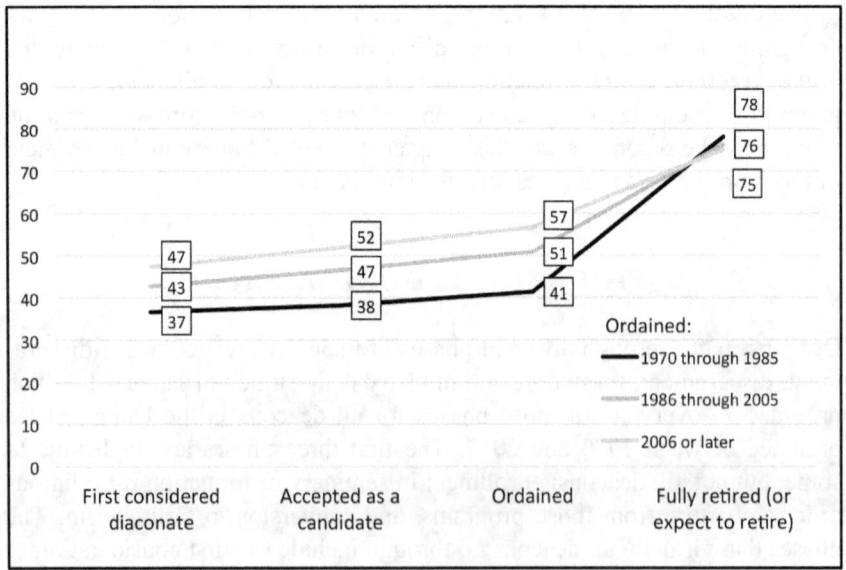

Figure 4.1. Age (in years) at different phases of a deacon's life by ordination cohort.
Graphic courtesy of the author.

in the youngest cohort (2006 or later). Those differences grow wider as deacons in each cohort progressed to candidacy and ordination, because deacons in the oldest cohort moved faster to ordination.

Notably, this trend reverses at retirement. The deacons in the oldest cohort retired or intend to do so at an average age of 78 as compared to 76 years old for those in the middle cohort and 75 for those in the youngest cohort. If deacons in the three cohorts were to keep their retirement plans, then there will be very significant differences in the amount of time each cohort spends in active ministry. Specifically, those ordained in the oldest cohort would serve as deacons for 37 years on average, those ordained in the middle cohort for 25 years, and those ordained in the youngest cohort for only 18 years. This is a significant difference—with deacons in the oldest cohort serving twice as long as those in the youngest cohort. This trend should be a major consideration in dioceses that opt for longer periods of pre-ordination formation, as well as for bishops in general when setting mandatory retirement ages for deacons, and when budgeting the costs of initial investment associated with pre-ordination formation.

Figure 4.2 further illustrates the decreasing trend in the amount of time deacons stayed (or intend to stay) in ministry.

In order to better understand the life cycle of deacons, the following subsections describe in greater detail each of the before-mentioned phases in deacons' formation, beginning with the decisions some deacons have to make prior to the initial discernment and concluding with retirement from ministry as a deacon.

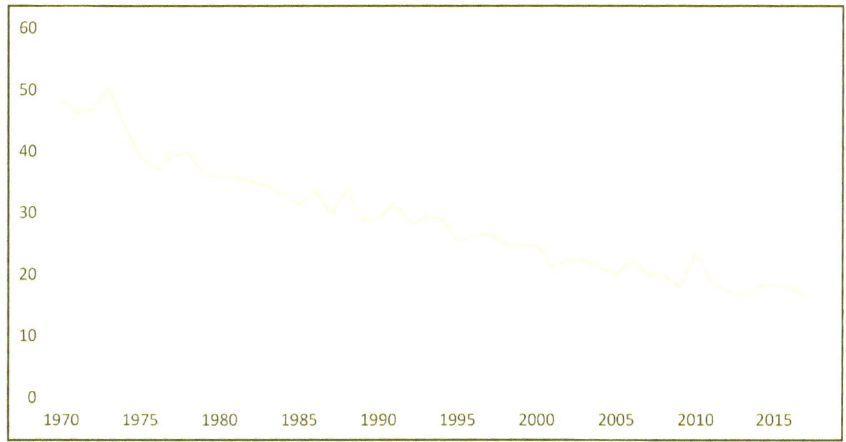

Figure 4.2. Time (in years) that deacons stayed (or intend to stay) in ministry by year of ordaination.

Graphic courtesy of the author.

Pre-discernment

Arguably, the path to the diaconate begins long before the first serious consideration of the vocation. The discernment of the vocation can only be made on the foundation of faith. Overall, 85 percent of all deacons were born Catholic (1 percent was of Eastern rite, while the other 84 percent are Latin rite). The remaining 15 percent converted to Catholicism later in life, on average, at 30 years old (a median of 28). The biggest share of deacon-converts can be found in the South (19 percent) and West (18 percent), followed by Midwest (15 percent), and Northeast (9 percent).

Religious education helps develop the faith that provides the foundation for the discernment of a diaconal vocation. As indicated in chapter 3, more than half of all deacons (63 percent) attended Catholic elementary/middle school, half (48 percent) attended Catholic high school, a third (32 percent) attended Catholic college or university on the undergraduate level, and a quarter (25 percent) attended on the graduate level.

Whether or not they attended Catholic schools, deacons also received much of their faith formation by participating in various activities. The most common Catholic formation activities were parish religious education programs (attended by 64 percent of deacons), followed by parish/diocesan youth ministry (39 percent), Catholic campus ministry (16 percent), and post-college volunteer service such as the Jesuit Volunteer Corps (5 percent). An in-depth description of those activities and education in general can be found in chapter 3.

Those activities and Catholic schooling may help prospective deacons grow in their faith and develop character traits that make future "exemplary deacons." According to the *Formation Directory*, those character traits include (but are not limited to) natural inclination to service, integrity, capacity for dialogue, respect for others (as opposed to prejudice), communication skills, kindness and humility, responsibility, as well as the ability to lead, motivate, facilitate, and animate others. The *Formation Directory* also mentions spiritual and evangelical qualities such as maturity and holiness, participation in the Church's sacramental life and involvement in the apostolate, as well as capacity for obedience and fraternal communion.

In addition to developing those qualities, to successfully discern and respond to the call to diaconate, prospective deacons need to be established in other areas of their lives. As the *Formation Directory* explains, there is "the element of readiness and the timeliness of one's response to a vocation. Since inquirers to the diaconate have many commitments to family, career, employment, community, and church service, it is a matter of prudential judgment to explore not only whether the call to the diaconate is from the Holy Spirit, but also whether the inquirer is ready and able to respond to that call at the present time" (2005: §168).

Personal Discernment

The *Formation Directory* identifies four phases in a typical process of discerning a call to diaconate: personal discernment, family discernment, communal discernment, and ecclesial discernment. Those phases likely overlap to a large extent. The first phase, personal discernment, usually begins "with seeking information about the diaconate and formation" and with individual reflection "upon the nature of [the] perceived call" (Bishops' Committee on the Diaconate 2005: §169).

This process of reflection is often convoluted, as illustrated by the fact that the majority of deacons discerned other vocations in addition to the diaconate. Three out of five deacons (61 percent) have considered becoming a priest or a religious brother. One in three deacons (33 percent) have been "somewhat" or "very" serious about it. It is not clear how discerning and pursuing the calling to diaconate relates to other vocations. It appears that it may precede, follow, or exist concurrently with other discernments, but the extent to which each of these scenarios occurs cannot be inferred from the available data.

Overall, 17 percent of deacons were at one point enrolled in a seminary or in formation for a religious order. Those deacons who enrolled in those programs did so at an average age of 17 (a median of 16). This indicates that the deacons in this group tended to enroll in minor seminaries (as opposed to college or major seminaries). This thesis is supported by the fact that, on average, the enrollments took place in 1965 and departures in 1969, during a period when minor seminaries were still relatively prevalent in the United States.

While enrollment in seminary or in formation for a religious order took place, on average, at a relatively young age, the serious consideration of the call to diaconate came typically at a much older age. On average, deacons say they first seriously considered becoming a deacon at age 44 (a median age of 45).[2] As mentioned earlier, deacons ordained in the oldest cohort (1970 through 1985) first considered the diaconate, on average, six years earlier than deacons ordained in the middle cohort (1986 through 2005) and 11 years earlier than those ordained in the youngest cohort (2006 or later).

Family Discernment

The second phase in a typical process of discerning a call to diaconate is family discernment. This includes prospective deacons discussing their possible

Table 4.2. Encouragement from others during discernment.

	"Somewhat" or "Very" Encouraging %	"Very" Encouraging %
Wife	95	79
Another priest/religious	95	78
A deacon	94	81
Pastor	93	77
Fellow parishioners	93	67
Children	85	49
Bishop	84	60
Mother	80	55
Other relatives	75	39
Father	72	48
Siblings	70	35
Coworkers	67	30
Neighbors	59	26

vocation with their wives and families. This also includes gathering initial information and early conversations with their pastor and others (Bishops' Committee on the Diaconate 2005). Table 4.2 quantifies the involvement of those close to the prospective deacons in their discernment process.

Almost all deacons (at least 96 percent) were married at the time when they were discerning their vocation to the diaconate. Since "[f]or a married man, the support and consent of his wife is required" (Bishops' Committee on the Diaconate 2005: §170; see also §70 and §138), it comes as no surprise that virtually all married prospective deacons who were accepted to the formation program (99 percent) felt at least "a little" encouraged to pursue the vocation by their wives and 79 percent felt "very" encouraged. Similarly, a vast majority of deacons (93 to 95 percent) is most likely to consider their pastors, deacons, and other priests or religious to be "somewhat" or "very" encouraging (as opposed to "not at all" or "only a little").

Depending on the culture and traditions specific to different regions, extended family and other acquaintances may also constitute an important resource for discernment (Bishops' Committee on the Diaconate 2005). Three types of deacons can be fairly well distinguished in this regard: deacons who were generally unlikely to receive encouragement, those in between, and those who were most likely to be surrounded by people "very" encouraging of the deacons' vocation. The first group, deacons who were generally unlikely to receive encouragement, constitutes 24 percent of the deacons. Deacons in this group typically report that fellow parishioners were "somewhat" encouraging and that their children were "only a little" encouraging. On the other hand, all other persons were most often "not" encouraging during deacons' discernment (either because those persons chose not to be encouraging or because those persons were not present in deacons' lives).

The second group of deacons received mixed amounts of encouragement from different persons in their lives. This group constitutes 43 percent of the deacons. Deacons in this group are most likely to state that they were "very" encouraged by their fellow parishioners, their bishops, and their mothers; that they were "somewhat" encouraged by their fathers, children, siblings, and other relatives; and that they were "only a little" encouraged by their coworkers and neighbors.

The third group of deacons is most likely to report that they were "very" encouraged to pursue their vocation by everyone. Those deacons constitute 34 percent of the responding deacons.

Communal Discernment

The third phase in a typical process of discerning a call to diaconate is communal discernment. As the *Formation Directory* explains, "[a]n inquiry and eventual application for entrance into diaconal formation is not just a personal and family journey. The Church must accompany it. The parish is the primary experience of Church for most inquirers. It is the responsibility of this community and, in particular, its pastor to invite from among its members those who may be qualified to serve as ordained ministers of the Church (Congregation for Catholic Education 1998). Similarly, those church and community agencies that have often carried out the Church's mission of charity and justice have a unique opportunity to call forth appropriate nominees from among their personnel" (2005: §171). According to Noll (2006), many deacons are active members in their parish communities before they begin studies for the diaconate, and these ecclesial communities play a strong role in the discernment of the diaconal vocation.

In general, the vast majority of deacons (93 percent) felt "somewhat" or "very" encouraged by their pastor and fellow parishioners during their discernment (as opposed to "not at all" or "only a little"). However, some deacons voiced their desire for stronger communal support, in particular regarding prayer support and attracting new vocations. Among the 2,214 deacons who provided open-ended comments regarding what they would most like to see improved regarding the diaconate, 68 deacons explicitly mentioned vocations. Deacons in this group pointed out that intercessory prayers for vocations and vocational materials should include vocations to the diaconate (in addition to vocations to the priesthood and religious life). One deacon shared his experience of trying to raise this issue just to be told that "deacons are a 'secondary vocation,' and not a 'real' vocation." Another deacon pointed out that excluding the deacons does not only have a detrimental effect on attracting new vocations, but also "devalues the vocation, orders received, and insults the bishop who confirmed the call to service."

Ecclesial Discernment

The fourth phase preceding formal formation in a typical process of discerning a call to diaconate is ecclesial discernment. At this phase, "an inquiry about the diaconate and the formation process (. . .) includes the diocesan Church. Information sessions, the exploration of the criteria for a diaconal vocation, and particular counsel presented by the diocesan diaconate office can aid an individual in his decision to move forward to a formal application" (Bishops' Committee on the Diaconate 2005: §172).

The formal process for admission into a diaconal formation program begins when a prospective deacon is presented by his pastor and submits an application. At this phase, "[b]oth the applicant and the diocesan Church enter into an intensive screening process" (2005: §173). A committee on admission and scrutinies reviews the applicant's abilities and potential for ordained ministry, explores for the presence of canonical impediments to ordination, and nominates applicants (§173, §175, §176, §284). The formation occurs through two distinct, yet related, processes. The first process leads to acceptance into the aspirant path. The second process leads to admittance into the candidate path in diaconal formation.

The applicant may be considered not suitable, suitable in the future, or suitable for admission into aspirancy pending bishop's approval. Once the applicant is accepted into aspirancy, the admission process continues with an assessment of readiness for entrance into the candidate path in formation (§181).

While the prospective deacon may successfully complete his discernment and the Church may deem him suitable for the diaconate, both processes continue until the ordination. And, in some cases, these processes may end with disappointing conclusions. One deacon provided an example of such a situation:

> *The problem: men can be engaged in the training and formation, and even up to the last few months be dismissed. I understand the need to discern God's call— and that this is a mutual issue, the candidate as well as the church. However, to invest seven or eight years in the process, and then be dismissed is heartbreaking. An earlier discernment effort, after two or three years, should be attempted.*

Anecdotes like this one may indicate that there is a need for more focused discernment and stricter application review practices in some dioceses.

Aspirancy

Once the initial inquiry process is completed, the bishop decides to accept prospective deacons into aspirancy, which in the diocesan churches of the United States ordinarily lasts one year (Bishops' Committee on the Diaconate 2005). Aspirancy is a "propaedeutic period" to discern the capability and readiness of an aspirant to be nominated to candidacy for diaconal ordination (Congregation for Catholic Education 1998; Bishops' Committee on the Diaconate 2005). The purpose of aspirancy is also to introduce prospective deacons to "the study of theology, to a deeper knowledge of the spirituality and ministry of the deacon, and to a more attentive discernment of his call (. . .), to introduce him to the pastoral ministries of the diocesan Church, and to assist his family in their support of his formation [Congregation for Catholic Education 1998: §41–44]" (Bishops' Committee on the Diaconate 2005: §187).

The formation during aspirancy introduces prospective deacons to a unified diocesan formation program for deacons that extends to candidacy and post-ordination. According to the *Formation Directory*, this program is intended to promote the development of the whole person. For this reason, this unified program is designed around four dimensions for a complete formation process:

- The human dimension focuses on the deacon's human formation and development by cultivating "a series of human qualities, not only out of proper and due growth and realization of self, but also with a view to the ministry" (Pope St. John Paul II 1992: §43 in Bishops' Committee on the Diaconate 2005: §106).
- The spiritual dimension focuses on the processes where the deacon is discerning and affirming the signs of his vocation.
- The intellectual dimension focuses on the deacon's understanding and ability to communicate the fundamental teachings of the Church.
- The pastoral dimension focuses on the deacon's developing pastoral experience.

To address the complications related to personal and family commitments as well as secular employment, "the most common formation models that have emerged in the United States organize formation meetings on various evenings, weekends, holidays, or a combination of such times" (Bishops' Committee on the Diaconate 2005: §185). Notably, "[t]he aspirant path also must enable the formation personnel to create an environment in which a wife of a married aspirant can be appropriately prepared to give her consent to his continuation, and more essentially, to ascertain her compatibility with her husband's diaconal vocation and eventual ministry [Congregation for Catholic Education 1998: §37]" (Bishops' Committee on the Diaconate 2005: §186).

Candidacy

The minimum age for admission to candidacy is left to the discretion of individual dioceses. According to Gautier and Holland (2017), 93 percent of dioceses in the United States have a minimum age for acceptance into a diaconate formation program, which is, on average, 33 years of age (a median of age 32). Furthermore, 78 percent of dioceses have a maximum age limit, which is, on average, 59 years of age (a median of 60).

In practice, deacons are typically accepted to candidacy and begin formation for the diaconate within one year, at an average age of 48 (a median of 49).[3] Notably, major differences exist between ordination cohorts. Deacons ordained in the oldest cohort (1970 through 1985) were accepted as candidates for the diaconate at an average age of 38. This is considerably younger than deacons ordained in the middle cohort (1986 through 2005), who were accepted as candidates for the diaconate at the age of 47 on average, and deacons ordained in the youngest cohort (2006 or later), who were accepted as candidates for the diaconate at the average age of 52.

Once admitted to candidacy, prospective deacons are supposed "to spend three years in a program" (can. 236). This is "in addition to the *propaedeutic period*" (Bishops' Committee on the Diaconate 2005: §205). However, in some dioceses, formation programs are designed to take considerably longer and some candidates may need significantly more time to complete the program. On average, deacons spend four years in diaconate formation (between one and twelve years).

The purpose of candidacy is "continued discernment of a diaconal vocation and immediate preparation for ordination" (§204). This purpose is in part accomplished through an extensive education program. According to the *Formation Directory*, the core curriculum should cover the following areas:

- Scripture (in particular, the biblical themes of justice and peace that root and foster Catholic social teaching);
- dogmatic theology (in particular, the Sacrament of Holy Orders as well as the theology and the relationship of the diaconate to the episcopate, the presbyterate, and the laity);
- moral theology (in particular, the social teaching of the Church);
- historical studies (in particular, patristics and multicultural origins of the Church in the United States);

- Canon Law (in particular, canons specific to marriage legislation, as well as the obligations and rights of clerics);
- spirituality;
- liturgy;
- practica for the ministry of liturgy;
- homiletics; and
- pastoral formation (in particular, the study of the role of culture in human and spiritual formation).

This comprehensive program is implemented in various formats. According to the *Formation Directory*, the formation program is supposed to include "not only class preparation, participation, and attendance, but also seminars, workshops, field education projects, theological reflection, shared opportunities for spiritual growth (e.g., liturgical celebrations and prayer, spiritual conferences, retreats), individual spiritual direction, and other formation experiences" (§206). Nine in ten deacons (88 percent) reported having a spiritual director in their formation.

Furthermore, some of the formation takes place in language(s) other than English. One in twenty deacons (6 percent) had at least some of their diaconate formation in a language other than English. Notably, deacons in the West (11 percent) were more likely than deacons in the South (6 percent), Midwest or Northeast (5 percent each) to encounter a language other than English during at least some of their formation.

On average, deacons spend 22 hours per month in pre-ordination formation (a median of 20 hours). In practice, the majority of the formation takes place in person. According to Gautier and Holland (2017), 31 percent of dioceses in the United States provide at least a portion of the academic formation of deacons through distance learning (15 percent through synchronous learning, 20 percent through asynchronous, and 5 percent in some other way).

Internet technology is utilized in diaconate formation to a limited extent. It appears that online formation was first employed more systematically with the ordination class of 2004, when five deacons reported utilizing it. One in eight deacons (13 percent) since that year received at least some diaconate formation online. Notably, the share of those ordained between 2004 and 2017 who relied on Internet technologies is higher in the South (18 percent) and West (15 percent) than in Midwest (10 percent) and Northeast (7 percent).

The formation program does not focus exclusively on the candidates, but also aims to incorporate their wives. As noted earlier, 99 percent of married deacons felt at least "a little" encouraged to pursue the vocation by their wives and 79 percent felt "very" encouraged. Nine in ten deacons' wives (86 percent) participated in their husbands' diaconate formation. Notably, wives in the West (92 percent) were significantly more likely to participate than wives in Midwest (86 percent), South (86 percent) or Northeast (84 percent).

Post-ordination

The minimum age for ordination in the United States is 35 for all candidates, married or celibate (Bishops' Committee on the Diaconate 2005). On average, deacons responding to the deacon survey were ordained at 52 years old (a median of 53). As noted earlier, deacons ordained in the oldest cohort (1970 through 1985) were ordained relatively younger, at an average age of 41. By comparison, those ordained in the middle cohort (1986 through 2006) were ordained at an average age of 51, and those in the youngest cohort (2006 or later) were ordained at an average age of 57. Given that the average age of deacons is currently 68 years old (a median of 68), deacons have an average of 16 years of experience in ministry as a deacon.

According to the *Formation Directory*, deacons should be able to attend a post-ordination program planned for the first three years of their diaconal ministry. A program for all deacons regardless of their experience should be designed annually. Furthermore, "[e]ach diocesan Church is to establish a basic minimum of continuing education hours to be fulfilled on an annual basis by all diocesan deacons in active service. This would be in addition to time allocated for the annual diaconal community retreat" (Bishops' Committee on the Diaconate 2005: §254).

Those guidelines are not always followed. According to Gautier and Holland (2017), deacons in 97 percent of dioceses in the United States are required to participate in an annual retreat and 89 percent require deacons to attend post-ordination formation, which takes an average of 21 hours (a median of 20).

A caveat should be added that deacons tend to be confused about the post-ordination formation requirement in their arch/diocese. Currently, active deacons in three quarters of dioceses (73 percent) gave conflicting responses about the existence of this requirement. In the remaining quarter of dioceses, all active deacons consistently report that they are required to undergo post-ordination formation. Despite tending to not know they are required to do so, the vast majority of active deacons (81 percent) have continued in a formal education program for ministry. On average, active deacons who continue in those programs participated in 30 hours of ongoing formation in the last year (a median of 20 hours). Furthermore, deacons in this group reported completing a median of one course every year-and-a-half since their ordination.

The purpose of post-ordination formation can be defined as "a process of continual conversion" (Congregation for the Clergy 1998: §65). According to the *Formation Directory*, the purposes of post ordination formation include: avoiding the risk of ministerial burnout, preventing conflict between deacons and their spouses and families, and providing specialized training to address particular needs of the people deacons serve.

Other practical purposes of post-formation programs reported by the deacons themselves include building social ties with each other, staying "alert intellectually," and learning in "areas only briefly covered (or not covered) during formation."

The post-ordination formation programs may be provided in various formats, such as: diocesan, regional, or national conferences, workshops and seminars, retreats, self-guided study, distance learning, ministry reflection groups, and mentoring groups (Bishops' Committee on the Diaconate 2005). The post-ordination formation can also include informal (as opposed to structured) support. For example, 80 percent of active deacons feel that they have someone they can confide in for issues related to ministry and 44 percent report having access to a support group.

Retirement

As noted in chapter 2, more than half of dioceses have a mandatory retirement policy for deacons in active ministry: about eight in ten dioceses require deacons to retire at age 75. Another tenth of dioceses set age 70 as a mandatory retirement age for deacons. On average, deacons fully retired (or expect to fully retire) from diaconal ministry at 76 (a median of 75).[4]

Deacons in the oldest cohort (ordained in 1970 through 1985) retired or intend to do so at an average age of 78, as compared to 76 years old for those in the middle cohort (1986 through 2005), and 75 years old for those in the youngest cohort (2006 or later). Of course, there is a possibility that deacons originally plan to retire earlier and, as the year of retirement gets closer, they may decide to postpone it. However, more than half of dioceses have a mandatory retirement policy for deacons in active ministry. Thus, the opposite may also happen—deacons planning to retire later may be required to retire earlier than they would prefer.

If deacons in the three ordination cohorts were to keep their retirement plans, then there would be very significant differences in the amount of time each cohort spends in active ministry. Specifically, those ordained in the oldest cohort would serve as deacons for 37 years on average, those ordained in the middle cohort for 25 years, and those ordained in the youngest cohort for only 18 years.

A number of questions arise regarding deacons' experience in retirement: do they feel supported and included in the life of their diocese? Do they have the financial means to retire with dignity after years of working in uncompensated ministry? Do they feel that they would like to continue in their ministry past the mandatory retirement age? While the open-ended comments hint that some of those areas may be problematic, the available data do not offer any answers. As more deacons reach retirement age, those questions will become increasingly important.

DEACONS' NEEDS REGARDING FORMATION

When asked about their needs regarding formation, deacons provided their assessment of the pre-ordination and post-ordination formation programs as well as suggested improvements to those programs. Many deacons also pointed out that, just as they need to be prepared for diaconal ministry in the Church, others in the Church would benefit from being educated about deacons and their role relative to the parish priests, lay parish employees, and to the faithful. Each of those areas is described below.

Assessment of Formation Programs

In general, deacons tend to feel well-prepared for their ministry. They also report being seen as competent by their supervising priests. Nine in ten active deacons feel that their formation and training adequately prepared them for ministry (87 percent) and that they have been placed in a position that matches their skill set (87 percent). Nine in ten (90 percent) feel trusted by their supervising priests.

Deacons are relatively unlikely to regularly receive evaluations, which could help focus the ongoing formation efforts. Less than half (40 percent) receive evaluations on their ministry on a regular basis. This appears to be a missed opportunity. According to the *Formation Directory*, "[a]ssessments are valuable occasions for the discernment, affirmation, and development of a participant's vocation. Assessments should be made and communicated on a regular basis" (2005: §70).

In general, the diaconate formation programs have been fairly comprehensive from the very beginning. Deacons ordained between 1973 and 1975 report that, on average, 11 to 12 topics (out of 14 identified topics in Table 4.3) were treated in their formation. Deacons ordained in all other years report that, on average, 13 to 14 of these topics were treated in their diaconate formation program.

Table 4.3. Deacons' rating of their formation program by topic.

	"Good" or "Excellent" %	"Excellent" Only %
Theological formation	93	51
Scriptural formation	89	49
Spiritual formation	88	50
Intellectual formation	86	40
Pastoral formation	83	37
Homiletics training	80	42
Personal/human development	79	33
Field experience	62	24
Counseling training	43	13
Liturgical training for special liturgies	42	14
Hospital ministry training	40	17
Prison ministry training	21	8
Emcee training for Masses with Bishop	16	5

Virtually all respondents received theological, spiritual, scriptural, and pastoral formation as well as homiletics training. On the other hand, the topics most likely to be reported as not covered in the formation program include: prison ministry training (reported as not treated in formation by 16 percent of all deacons), emcee training for Masses with Bishop (12 percent), hospital ministry training (9 percent), and counseling training (5 percent).

In general, deacons positively assess their diaconate formation program. On average, deacons ordained every year between 1970 and 2017 rate the quality of their diaconate formation programs as "good" (as opposed to "poor," "only fair," or "excellent"). The deacons ordained at the beginning of this period (1970 to 1972) and at the very end (2017) rate their programs slightly more positively, on average.

Notably, some deacons stated that education and formation has improved over the years since they were ordained. As one deacon put it:

As a member of the very first class in our diocese, we were perhaps a "trial and error" program. I am very much encouraged by the structure and implementation of the deaconate formation we now have in our diocese. [Men currently being ordained] are extremely well prepared for their role as ordained deacons.

The topics most likely to be rated "good" or "excellent" (as opposed to "poor" or "only fair") include theological, scriptural, spiritual, and intellectual formation (each being rated as "good" or "excellent" by at least nine in ten deacons). On the other hand, more than half of the deacons rated several areas as "poor" or "only fair:" counseling training, liturgical training for special liturgies, hospital ministry training, prison ministry training, and emcee training for Masses with Bishop.

Suggested Improvements to Formation Programs

When asked about what they would most like to see improved in the permanent diaconate, one in five deacons who offered a response (21 percent) focused on the issues pertaining to vocation, formation, retreats, and/or preparation. One deacon summed up his preparation for ministry by stating that the pre-ordination "education was 'excellent,' but practical experience upon ordination was lacking," and the parish priest was not educated on how to work with a deacon. In general, many deacons stated that their pre-ordination formation would benefit from more practical preparation. As one deacon put it:

> *Most [formation] programs lead to a degree in Theology or Philosophy but this, while laudable, does not address the day-to-day work of the deacon as a "servant."*

A closely related problem is, in the view of some deacons, that the formation is becoming "too academic," which in some cases may result in "good men who (. . .) would be very good at showing the face of Christ to their communities" not being able to become deacons, because they "do not meet the academic requirements."

Notably, many priests also feel that their seminary formation does not include sufficient hands-on preparation (e.g., Conway 1992, 2002, Hoge 2002, 2006). This hints at a more wide-spread perception of deficiency in the educational system responsible for the formation and training of the clergy in the United States in regards to applied training. A caveat should be added that major differences may exist across dioceses in their formation programs for both priests and deacons.

Many deacons believe that it would be helpful to improve the quantity and quality of formation opportunities. Their main suggestions for specific improvements include covering areas already listed in the *Formation Directory* and tend to focus on a need for developing practical skills. This suggests that the problem does not lie in identifying areas important to the formation of deacons but in effectively implementing education in those areas.

Some deacons called for developing a standard curriculum that could be used uniformly across the United States. At least one deacon called for developing "formation on par with seminarians." Additionally, some deacons suggested integrating pre-ordination and post-ordination formation, as well as programming for priests and deacons as a way of fostering new relationships, sharing experiences, increasing the recognition of the deacons as clergy and as a way of decreasing ambiguity about the deacons' role and decreasing the tension between deacons and priests.

Those suggestions may conflict with preferences voiced by some deacons, who would like the programming to be custom tailored to particular groups of deacons (e.g., post-formation programs for working deacons), and greater flexibility in post-ordination education (e.g., by individually developing "a continuing education plan that is approved by the Director of the Diaconate and/or the bishop"). In regard to one-on-one attention, a number of deacons expressed the need for "[i]ncreased availability of Spiritual Directors both pre- and post-formation."

Implementing those suggestions would likely lead to more administrative burden. This is a problem considering that some deacons noted that some formation programs may have already reached administrative capacity. As one deacon stated:

Our current Deacon Director has virtually no interaction with the deacons and spends his time only with those in formation. We need two directors, one for formation and one for ordained, or a different director who is exclusively employed by the diocese.

Some deacons voiced a preference for more extensive curricula. In conflict with this view are deacons in dioceses with longer formation programs who advocated for shortening the length of those programs or replacing some classes with training in the parish. For example, one deacon argued that:

The length of formation in my current diocese is five years. For married men who are also holding jobs this is discouraging.

Deacons are also divided in regard to the criteria for admitting candidates to diaconal formation. A few deacons made observations regarding the demographic make-up of the candidates to diaconate. For example, one deacon stated a need for "[m]ore African American men accepted as candidates into formation." Another indicated a need for more deacons who can serve in the fast-growing Hispanic community.[5]

On the other hand, one deacon cautioned against increasing the quantity of deacons in those most-needed areas at the expense of the quality of the ministry they can provide. As he explained:

I have seen so many exceptions (lowering of the bar) on the acceptance process because of the desire to have more deacons of a particular race or culture. When this variation of deacons interacts with the people of God, the message and teachings of the church are not consistent.

Some deacons expressed a desire for more opportunities for feedback and for participation in designing formation programs. One deacon explained it this way:

A more collegial atmosphere would be welcome. Directors of the Diaconate (several directors since my ordination) make rules, add requirements and hold an annual archdiocesan deacon retreat (but not like a true "retreat") in which new policies and issues are given without input, discussion and (it seems) respect for the opinions of the deacons.

Finally, a caveat should be added that when considering the improvements to formation programs described here, one should keep in mind that while some enhancements may appear desirable in theory, they may not be practical. For example, as one deacon observed, "realistically when functions are organized, most consider themselves too busy to participate."

Education about Deacons

In the opinion of many deacons, they and their wives are not the only ones in need of education and formation. As described in chapter 1, the diaconate in the early Church suffered from ambiguity about the deacons' roles and a tension between deacons and presbyters. While the underlying causes might be largely different, many deacons today report a lack of general understanding about their role by others and speak of the tension between deacons and their wives on one side and priests, lay church employees, bishops, and the faithful on the other side.

Deacons also report difficulties in finding support from some bishops and feeling that bishops are drawing a division between priests and deacons to, then, take the priests' side. One deacon observed that "[o]ften when bishops address a group of deacons they refer to bishops and priests as 'us' but when referring to the deacon they use the term 'you,' thereby excluding deacons." A few deacons mentioned that some bishops are hesitant to ordain deacons at all or ordain more deacons (in particular, to prevent the number of deacons exceeding the number of priests in the diocese).

Some deacons report major differences between priests and bishops with whom they work. While some priests and bishops make deacons feel "included and valued" others are more difficult. Generally, deacons tend to find younger priests more understanding of deacons' role than the older ones. Furthermore, in the opinion of some deacons, international priests tend to be harder to work with, because of cultural differences, but also because those priests often come from countries where the diaconate is not as prevalent, if present at all.

In general, the difficulties in the relationship between deacons and parish priests appear to stem from two general problems: priests not knowing how to work with deacons and priests not wanting to work with deacons. In regard to the first problem, one deacon states that priests he has encountered still do not know what to do with deacons. Another one suggested that:

Priests need to be taught how to use deacons most effectively in their parish and they need to learn how to let go of certain responsibilities without feeling like they are not doing their job.

Some deacons seem to believe that priests intentionally make their relationship difficult. One deacon observed that "[s]ometimes at the convocations it seems like an us/them or we/they relation rather than a coordinated unit serving the people of God." A few deacons accused some priests of being not sufficiently "respectful" or "accepting," of being "resentful," and "jealous," of "feeling threatened," as well as of being not "welcoming," not "caring," "ignorant, or outright reluctant to share ministry." One deacon stated that "[t]here are some priests averse to the ministry of deacons, and each of us [deacons] can relate horror stories."

Notably, not all deacons saw the problem of building a good working relationship as a function of priests' ignorance or negative attitude. For example, one deacon stated that he "would like to see more deacons being understanding about and supportive of priests, particularly young priests."

Some deacons also report difficulties in working with Church lay employees (such as parish staff) who may not understand deacons' status as clergy and who may not be sufficiently considerate of deacons' obligations to their families and secular employers. For example, one deacon stated that:

I think that while the priests I have served with understand that I already have a full-time job and family obligations, lay church employees are sometimes less understanding of this.

One example of this lack of understanding can be found in planning diocesan activities (such as convocations). For example, one deacon reported that those activities need to be planned more considerately of "those who work full-time outside of the Church and have to take time off from work to attend these events while church employees are on the clock."

Finally, some deacons feel that the faithful in general need to be educated about the role of deacons. Many of the deacons who feel this way seem to perceive that the problem of understanding and recognizing deacons is related to deacons being denied certain outward symbols of their clerical status. For example, one deacon stated that in some areas deacons are discouraged from wearing clerics. Another deacon stated that:

> There is a bias against permanent deacons viz-à-viz transitional deacons. We are denied the use of "Rev. Mr." but transitional deacons are always "Rev. Mr."

Notably, while deacons' roles in general (and in their parish community, in particular) may be ambiguous and under-appreciated, the role of deacons' wives may escape notice altogether. This important issue is explored in-depth in chapter 7.

CONCLUSION

In conclusion, it takes a lot to be a deacon. It takes a considerable amount of faith formation, character development, and growth in spiritual and evangelical qualities. It requires that one is established in other areas of his life (such as family and work life) in order to be able to respond to that call. It generally requires successfully completing a pre-ordination formation program and it takes ongoing formation efforts. It requires carrying out ministry in an environment where one may not feel understood by others.

Being a deacon may also require some sacrifices or challenges in family life, in career opportunities, and in free time. Those challenges can be organized into three overlapping groups:

- Challenges related to managing time: deacons spend an average of 19 hours per week on their ministry and 30 hours a year on ongoing formation. They also have various family obligations (e.g., 10 percent have children or stepchildren under age 18 currently living with them) and secular jobs (where they spend 39 hours a week, on average).
- Challenges related to supporting themselves: three-quarters of active deacons (74 percent) are not compensated for their ministry and deacons are often required to personally cover some of the expenses associated with their formation and ministry.
- Challenges related to emotional well-being: diaconal ministry may have some negative consequences on a deacon's family life. According to 39 percent of active deacons, their wives and/or children sometimes feel judged by others due to their ministry. Furthermore, 31 percent of all active deacons have difficulty balancing their home life and ministry.

If it takes so much to be a deacon, why have so many men in the United States answered the call? The answer to this question is explored in the next two chapters. Chapter 5 investigates what deacons do in their ministries and chapter 6 details deacons' satisfaction with their life and ministry.

NOTES

1. The first permanent deacon in the United States was ordained in 1969 and the first formation programs were operating by 1971 (Ditewig 2006).

2. By comparison, Gray and Gautier (2004) found that all deacons in 2001 first considered becoming a deacon one year earlier (an average age of 43 and median age of 42).

3. By comparison, Gray and Gautier (2004) found that all deacons in 2001 were accepted as candidates for the diaconate two years earlier (at an average age of 46, a median of 46).

4. A few responses above 100 were excluded from the analysis.

5. In general, the Church recognizes that there are some areas where diaconal ministry is more needed than in others. For example, U.S. Bishops' Committee on the Permanent Diaconate (1971) offers guidelines related to diaconal service in four types of communities: the black community, the Spanish-speaking community, the rural community, as well as on college and university campuses. The current *Formation Directory* states that the Hispanic Catholic population is of particular importance (§162).

Chapter Five

What Do the Deacons Do?
The Ministries of Deacons
Thu T. Do, LHC, and Michal J. Kramarek

Deacons have a multitude of responsibilities related to their families, secular jobs, and ministry. Notably, those responsibilities are related in that deacons carry out their ministry within the institutions of the Church, but also in their "private" lives, for example, in their family, work place, or at school (John Paul II 1993). Deacons' ministry is three-fold and includes Ministry of the Word, Ministry of Liturgy, and Ministry of Charity. Deacons carry out their ministry in many settings, but they are most frequently assigned to a parish for at least some of their ministry. The purpose of this chapter is to describe each of these three aspects of deacons' ministry, using the most recent empirical data from the 2017 national survey of deacons in the United States.

TIME SPENT IN MINISTRY

Overall, deacons spend an average of 19 hours per week on their ministry (a median of 15 hours) and 39 hours in a secular job (see Table 5.1). Since deacons may minister while working in their secular jobs, the overall amount spend on both activities might be less than the sum of time spend on each activity.

Notably, some deacons do not spend any time on ministry. This group may include deacons who are retired from ministry and deacons who are active but currently are not involved in any ministry (e.g., due to secular work relocation out of diocese). On the other end are deacons who spend as many as 100 hours a week preparing and carrying out their ministry. This group may include deacons who are on call or who live in places where they minister.

Table 5.1. Hours per week in diaconal ministry and in secular job by deacon's secular employment status (responses from all deacons).

	Diaconal Ministry			Secular Job		
	Mean	Median	Range	Mean	Median	Range
Working full-time	16	12	0–100	45	45	0–80
Working part-time	20	15	2–70	20	20	2–68
Retired	20	16	0–85	—	—	—
Not employed	25	20	0–78	—	—	—
All	19	15	0–100	39	40	0–80

Nine in ten deacons (87 percent) are currently active in ministry. Active deacons spend, on average, 20 hours per week serving in ministry, with half spending 15 hours or less. By comparison, in 2001, deacons spent an average of 23 hours per week in ministry with half spending 20 hours or less (Gray and Gautier 2004).

The deacons who are not employed in secular jobs average more time on their ministry (25 hours a week) than do deacons with secular employment. One in twenty-five deacons (4 percent) belongs to this group. By comparison, one in ten deacons (9 percent) is working part-time, spends, on average, 20 hours in their secular job and 20 hours a week on their ministry. Half of the deacons (51 percent) are retired from secular employment and spend, on average, 20 hours a week on their ministry. Finally, one-third of the deacons (32 percent) is employed full-time in a secular job and spends, on average, 45 hours in his secular job and 16 hours a week in his ministry.

It should be noted that deacons who receive compensation for their diaconal ministry spend more hours per week on average in that ministry than those who do not receive compensation (deacons compensated full-time spend 37 hours per week in ministry, those compensated part-time spend 23 hours per week in ministry, and those not compensated at all spend 17 hours per week in ministry).

In addition to spending time in ministry and secular employment, deacons spend time in post-ordination formation. Active deacons who continue in educational programs after ordination participate, on average, in 30 hours of ongoing formation (a median of 20 hours) in a year.

Many deacons also have demanding family obligations. Among active deacons, 10 percent have under-age children currently living with them. Some deacons report other important responsibilities that demand their time. For example, one deacon reported that "[t]here are a number of Deacons who have other obligations, like babysitting grandchildren and assisting their own parents."

PARISH MINISTRY

From the beginning, when the diaconate was originally restored as a stable and permanent order of ministry, deacons' ministry was typically connected to parish work. According to the document that established canonical norms for the renewed diaconate, one function of deacons is to "guide legitimately, in the name of the parish priest and of the bishop, remote Christian communities" (Pope Paul VI 1967: §21.10). This function is extended to also include leading parishes where priests are not available (can. 517 §2).

Deacons may also serve in parishes where priests are available. For example, deacons may support parish priests by contributing to the lives of parishes in densely populated areas by creating smaller groups that "can restore a family atmosphere, a fraternal warmth, to groups suffering from overgrowth" (Suenens 1985: 49).

Notably, the deacons' role in parishes is not limited to increasing the quantity of available clergy. Deacons may often be able to also increase the quality of ministry, especially in new areas of the Church's activity. According to Hypher, "[a] properly restored diaconate, where deacons are clearly seen to be part of the normal church community, will allow for professionalism and expertise in areas of diaconal work—essential in our scientific society, facing problems of technological importance" (1985: 43).

Currently, almost all deacons (98 percent) carry out at least some part of their ministry in parishes and 29 percent are engaged exclusively in parish ministry (see Figure 5.1). Among active deacons who do at least a part of their ministry in a parish, 79 percent serve at one parish, 20 percent serve in two or three parishes, and 2 percent serve in more than three parishes. Dea-

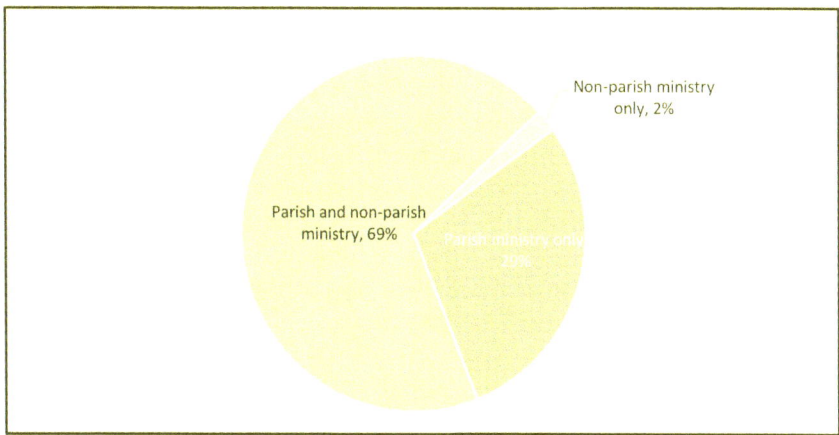

Figure 5.1. Active deacons' involvement in parish ministry.
Graphic courtesy of the author.

cons served in parish ministry for 14 years on average (a median of 12 years). As noted in chapter 4, deacons, on average, have 16 years of experience in ordained ministry. Very few deacons (3 percent), have served in a parish for a year or less.

Active deacons who were ordained in 2006 or later are 2 to 3 percentage points more likely than the two older ordination cohorts to serve in non-parish ministry exclusively. Active deacons not compensated for their ministry are 9 percentage points more likely than those in compensated ministry to minister exclusively in parish(es).

COMPENSATED MINISTRY

Diaconal ministry takes time and energy that could be otherwise exerted towards improving deacons' financial situation. Since deacons often carry most or all of the burden of expenses associated with their formation and ministry, the diaconate may further affect their financial situation. On average, 15 percent of active deacons nationwide feel that their ministry places a financial strain on their family. Furthermore, 9 percent of all active deacons feel that their ministry has impaired their advancement in their secular job.

According to the Church's rules regarding the compensation of deacons, "[m]arried deacons who devote themselves completely to ecclesiastical ministry deserve remuneration by which they are able to provide for the support of themselves and their families. Those who receive remuneration by reason of a civil profession which they exercise or have exercised, however, are to take care of the needs of themselves and their families from the income derived from it" (can. 281 §3). Furthermore, deacons may receive a salary if they hold some additional diocesan or parish position. For example, if a deacon is assigned to a parish, he does not typically receive a salary from the parish, but if he heads a diocesan office, he draws the salary associated with the office (Ditewig 2006). In practice, a quarter of all active deacons (26 percent) are compensated for their ministry. In this group, 59 percent are in a part-time and 41 percent in a full-time compensated ministry position.

The proportion of deacons who receive income for their work in the service of the Church has been relatively consistent over time. According to Gray and Gautier (2004), 27 percent of all active deacons in 2001 were compensated for their ministry, nearly identical to the 26 percent of active deacons in compensated ministry in 2017.

Among active deacons in compensated ministry, more than half (54 percent) serve in parishes (Figure 5.2), followed by deacons working in chancery

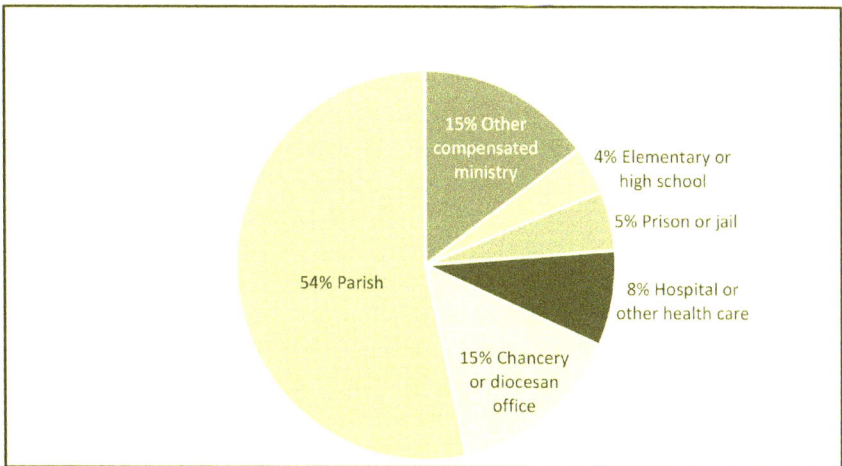

Figure 5.2. Active deacons in compensated ministry by type of compensated ministry.
Graphic courtesy of the author.

or diocesan offices (15 percent), in hospital ministry or other health care institutions (8 percent), in prison or jail settings (5 percent), in elementary or high schools (4 percent), or in other settings (such as military chaplaincy, retreat centers/houses of prayer, social service agencies, or colleges/universities).

There is one significant difference among ordination cohorts in the distribution of compensated ministries: compensated deacons who were ordained in 2006 or later are 5 percentage points more likely than those ordained between 1970 and 1985 to minister in an elementary or high school. Another significant difference can be found among geographic regions: compensated deacons living in the Northeast are 7 to 8 percentage points more likely than those in other areas of the country to minister in prisons and jails.

The pay scale for deacons in compensated positions is most often set by the deacons' parish (46 percent of deacons function under such an arrangement). In a quarter of the cases (26 percent), the pay sale is set by the diocese, and in the remaining quarter (24 percent) by the organization where a deacon ministers. Furthermore, half of the ministry positions have a formal ministerial contract (47 percent), and two-thirds of the ministry positions have a formal job description.

Not only are the majority of deacons not compensated for their ministry, most are also required to pay the expenses associated with their ministry, including expenses for formation. According to Gautier and Holland (2017), deacons are required to pay, on average, 35 percent of the cost of post-ordination formation programs (which are required in 89 percent of dioceses and eparchies), and a similar proportion of the cost of retreats (that are required by 97 percent of dioceses and eparchies).

Not surprisingly, some deacons do not believe this is fair. For example, one deacon put it this way: "Over the years, I [have] never received and never been offered compensation. It's an insult to then have to pay our own way [to] attend [mandatory] continuing education, retreats, gala dinners, etc."

THE THREE-FOLD MINISTRY OF DEACONS

As described in depth in chapter 1, deacons perform a wide range of functions, balanced between the three ministerial areas of word, sacrament, and pastoral service (Bishops' Committee on the Diaconate 2005). According to the Congregation for the Clergy, the three areas are interconnected: "the ministry of the word leads to ministry at the altar, which in turn prompts the transformation of life by the liturgy, resulting in charity" (1998: §39).

The ministry of the word focuses on proclaiming and illustrating the word of God (Pope St. John Paul II 1985), proclaiming the scriptures as well as instructing and exhorting the people (Congregation for Catholic Education 1998). The ministry of liturgy or sacrament focuses on administering the selected sacraments (Pope St. John Paul II 1985) and the sacramentals (Congregation for Bishops 2004), as well as assisting in various liturgical functions (Kwatera 2005). Finally, the ministry of charity or service can be understood as "the ministry of love and justice" (Bishops' Committee on the Diaconate 1985) that focuses on carrying out works of charity and assistance (Congregation for Catholic Education 1998) by serving as a community animator, by serving in ecclesial life (Pope St. John Paul II 1985), as well as by serving in those areas relating to the exercise of charity and the administration of goods (Congregation for Bishops 2004).

Among the three types of ministry, active deacons spend the most time in the ministry of charity—an average of seven hours per week. By comparison, active deacons spend six hours a week on average in the ministry of

Table 5.2. Hours per week active deacons spend in various aspects of ministry.

	Mean	Median	Range*
Ministry of Liturgy	5	4	0–64
Ministry of the Word	6	4	0–70
Ministry of Charity	7	5	0–100
Other ministry	10	5	0–70

*The maximum value of a response was limited to 100 hours a week.

the word and five hours in the ministry of liturgy. Notably, active deacons also spend ten hours a week in other ministry activities that cannot be easily classified into one of the three types. Examples of those other activities include administrative work, management, and professional services for the benefit of the parish.

Ministry of the Word

Deacons participate in evangelization and teaching in the Church's mission of heralding the Word. Some of the ways that deacons participate in this mission, for example, is in providing "catechetical instruction; religious formation of candidates and families preparing for the reception of the sacraments; leadership roles in retreats, evangelization, and renewal programs; outreach to alienated Catholics; and counseling and spiritual direction [Congregation for Catholic Education 1998: §86]" (Bishops' Committee on the Diaconate 2005: §31).

On average, deacons report spending nearly six hours a week on the ministry of the word. Two in three deacons (67 percent) spend one to five hours per week in this ministry, while a quarter (25 percent) spend six to ten hours. The remaining 8 percent average more than ten hours a week on the ministry of the word.

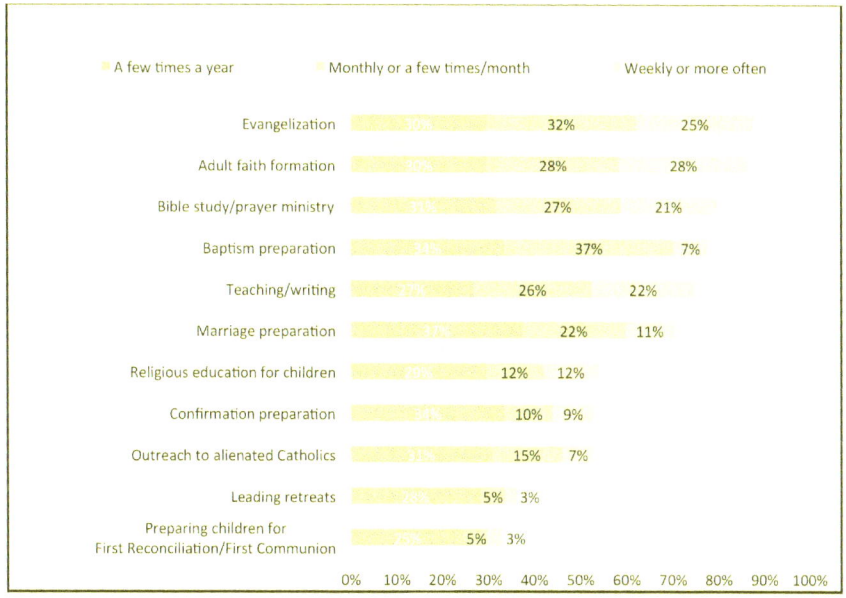

Figure 5.3. Active deacons' involvement in forms of ministry of the word.
Graphic courtesy of the author.

The ministry of the word can take many different forms. Figure 5.3 shows the approximate proportion of time that active deacons report spending in each of these various forms of ministry of the word. The most common among these forms is *evangelization*: reported by 88 percent of active deacons, a quarter (25 percent) say that they are engaged in evangelization at least once a week. Active deacons who are compensated are 5 percentage points more likely than those who are not compensated to be involved in this ministry and 5 percentage points more likely to do it frequently (i.e., at least weekly).

Adult faith formation is reported by 86 percent of active deacons; 28 percent are engaged in this at least once a week. Active deacons who are married are 6 percentage points more likely than those who are not married to be involved in this ministry, and 8 percentage points more likely to do it frequently. Active deacons working exclusively in parish(es) are 24 percentage points more likely than those not working in parish(es) to be involved in this ministry. Active deacons living in the South are 5 percentage points more likely than those in the Northeast to be involved in this ministry, and 5 percentage points more likely to do it frequently.

Bible study/prayer ministry is engaged in by 80 percent of active deacons; 21 percent conduct Bible study or some other prayer ministry at least once a week. Active deacons who are compensated are 6 percentage points more likely than those who are not compensated to be involved in this ministry. Active deacons not working in parish(es) are 12 percentage points more likely than those working exclusively in parish(es) to frequently engage in this ministry. Active deacons living in the South are 6 percentage points more likely than those in the Northeast to frequently engage in this ministry.

Baptism preparation is performed by 78 percent of active deacons; 7 percent do baptism preparation at least once a week and 37 percent do it monthly or a few times a month. Active deacons who were ordained between 1986 and 2005 are 4 percentage points more likely than those who were ordained in 2006 or later to frequently engage in this ministry. Active deacons who are married are 7 percentage points more likely than those who are not married to be involved in this ministry. Active deacons working exclusively in parish(es) are 33 percentage points more likely than those not working in parish(es) to be involved in this ministry. Active deacons living in the Northeast and the West are 10 percentage points more likely than those in the Midwest to be involved in this ministry.

Three in four active deacons (75 percent) are engaged in *teaching/writing*; 22 percent are teaching/writing at least once a week. Active deacons who are compensated are 8 percentage points more likely than those who are not compensated to be involved in this ministry and 10 percentage points more likely to do it frequently. Active deacons living in the West are 8 percentage points more likely than those in the Northeast to be involved in this ministry.

Marriage preparation is conducted by 70 percent of active deacons; 11 percent are engaged in marriage preparation at least once a week. Active deacons who were ordained between 1986 and 2005 are 3 percentage points more likely than those who were ordained in 2006 or later to be involved in this ministry. Active deacons who are married are 11 percentage points more likely than those who are not married to be involved in this ministry. Active deacons who are compensated are 6 percentage points more likely than those who are not compensated to be involved in this ministry, and 5 percentage points more likely to do it frequently. Active deacons working exclusively in parish(es) are 26 percentage points more likely than those not working in parish(es) to be involved in this ministry. Active deacons living in the South are 5 percentage points more likely than those in the Northeast to frequently engage in this ministry.

More than half of active deacons (54 percent) are engaged in *religious education for children*; 12 percent do this at least once a week. Active deacons in the two younger ordination cohorts are 6 percentage points more likely than those who were ordained between 1970 and 1985 to be involved in this ministry. Active deacons who are compensated are 8 percentage points more likely than those who are not compensated to frequently engage in this ministry. Active deacons working exclusively in parish(es) are 31 percentage points more likely than those not working in parish(es) to be involved in this ministry, and 10 percentage points more likely to do it frequently. Active deacons living in the Midwest and the Northeast are 10 percentage points more likely than those in the West to be involved in this ministry. Active deacons living in the Northeast are 7 percentage points more likely than those in the West to frequently engage in this ministry.

Outreach to alienated Catholics is reported by 53 percent of active deacons; 7 percent do such outreach at least once a week. Active deacons who are married are 9 percentage points more likely than those who are not married to be involved in this ministry. Active deacons who are compensated are 7 percentage points more likely than those who are not compensated to be involved in this ministry. Active deacons not working in parish(es) are 24 percentage points more likely than those working exclusively in parish(es) to be involved in this ministry and 15 percentage points more likely to do it frequently.

Confirmation preparation is conducted by 53 percent of active deacons; 9 percent are engaged in Confirmation preparation at least once a week. Active deacons who are compensated are 11 percentage points more likely than those who are not compensated to be involved in this ministry and 4 percentage points more likely to do it frequently. Active deacons working exclusively in parish(es) are 22 percentage points more likely than those not working in parish(es) to be involved in this ministry. Active deacons living in the Northeast and the South are 8 to 10 percentage points more likely than those in the Midwest to be involved in this ministry.

More than a third of active deacons (36 percent) are involved in *leading retreats*; 3 percent do this at least once a week). Active deacons who are compensated are 11 percentage points more likely than those who are not compensated to be involved in this ministry.

Preparing children for First Reconciliation/First Communion is conducted by 33 percent of active deacons; 3 percent do this at least once a week. Active deacons who are compensated are 10 percentage points more likely than those who are not compensated to be involved in this ministry. Active deacons working exclusively in parish(es) are 18 percentage points more likely than those not working in parish(es) to be involved in this ministry.

Ministry of Liturgy

Deacons also carry out many functions related to the ministry of liturgy. In general, those functions may include administering sacraments (with the exception of Eucharist and reconciliation), administering sacramentals, and assisting in various liturgical functions. Particularly noteworthy are the liturgical functions that relate to the deacons' ministry of charity. Those functions may include, for example, voicing the needs of the people in the General Intercessions at Mass and assisting the presider in accepting the offerings of the people, which is symbolic of deacons' "traditional role in receiving and distributing the resources of the community among those in need" (Bishops' Committee on the Diaconate 2005: §35).

On average, active deacons spend five hours per week on the ministry of liturgy (a median of four hours per week). Seven in ten deacons (69 percent) spend one to five hours per week in this ministry. A quarter (25 percent) report six to ten hours per week involved in the ministry of liturgy, and 6 percent spend more than ten hours per week in this aspect of ministry.

The ministry of liturgy can take many different forms. Figure 5.4 shows the approximate proportion of time that active deacons report spending in each of these various forms of ministry of liturgy. The form that is most familiar to parishioners and most commonly reported among deacons is *assisting at Mass*. Virtually all active deacons (99 percent) do this; 88 percent report doing this at least once a week. Active deacons in the two younger ordination cohorts are 3 percentage points more likely than those who were ordained between 1970 and 1985 to be involved in this ministry. Active deacons in

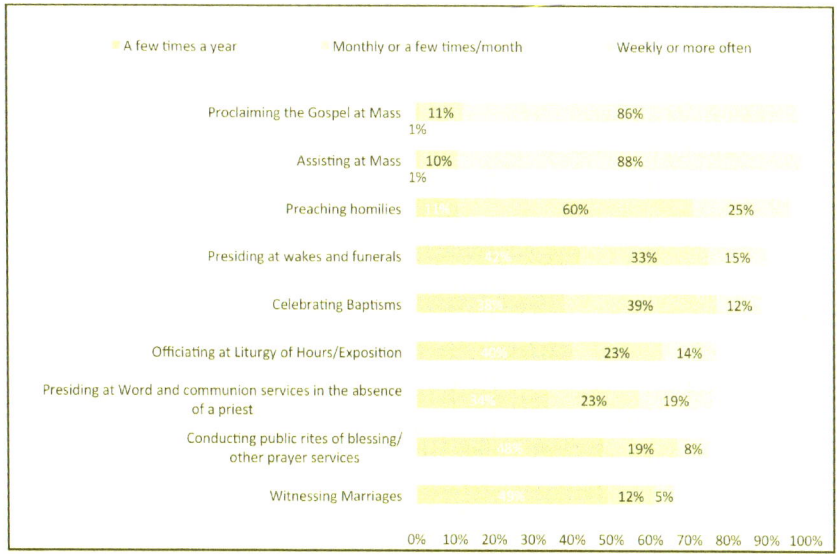

Figure 5.4. Active deacons' involvement in forms of ministry of liturgy.
Graphic courtesy of the author.

the two younger ordination cohorts are also 6 to 10 percentage points more likely than those who were ordained between 1970 and 1985 to say they engage in this ministry at least weekly. Active deacons working exclusively in parish(es) are 16 percentage points more likely than those not working in parish(es) to be involved in this ministry and 47 percentage points more likely to do it frequently. Active deacons living in the Northeast and the South are 6 to 12 percentage points more likely than those in the Midwest and the West to frequently engage in this ministry.

Proclaiming the Gospel at Mass is another form of the ministry of liturgy that is reported by virtually all active deacons (99 percent); 86 percent report doing this at least once a week. Active deacons in the two younger ordination cohorts are 2 percentage points more likely than those who were ordained between 1970 and 1985 to be involved in this ministry. Active deacons who were ordained in 2006 or later are 8 percentage points more likely than those who were ordained between 1970 and 1985 to frequently engage in this ministry. Active deacons who are compensated are 4 percentage points more likely than those who are not compensated to frequently engage in this ministry. Active deacons working exclusively in parish(es) are 14 percentage points more likely than those not working in parish(es) to be involved in this ministry and 38 percentage points more likely to do it frequently. Active deacons living in the Northeast are 11 percentage points more likely than those in the Midwest to frequently engage in this ministry. Active deacons living in the South are 9 percentage points more likely than those in the Midwest to frequently engage in this ministry.

Preaching homilies is reported by 96 percent of active deacons; 25 percent do it at least once a week. Active deacons who were ordained in 2006 or later are 5 percentage points more likely than those who were ordained between 1970 and 1985 to be involved in this ministry. Active deacons who were ordained between 1986 and 2005 are 6 percentage points more likely than those who were ordained in 2006 or later to frequently engage in this ministry. Active deacons who are compensated are 2 percentage points more likely than those who are not compensated to be involved in this ministry and 9 percentage points more likely to do it frequently. Active deacons working exclusively in parish(es) are 8 percentage points more likely than those not working in parish(es) to be involved in this ministry. Active deacons living in the Northeast are 9 percentage points more likely than those in the Midwest to frequently engage in this ministry. Active deacons living in the West are 10 percentage points more likely than those in the Midwest to frequently engage in this ministry.

Presiding at wakes and funerals is a form of the ministry of liturgy that is reported by 90 percent of active deacons; 15 percent do this ministry at least once a week. Active deacons who were ordained between 1986 and 2005 are 4 percentage points more likely than those who were ordained in 2006 or later to be involved in this ministry. Active deacons in the two older ordination cohorts are 8 to 12 percentage points more likely than those who were ordained in 2006 or later to frequently engage in this ministry. Active deacons who are not married are 12 percentage points more likely than those who are married to frequently engage in this ministry. Active deacons who are compensated are 4 percentage points more likely than those who are not compensated to be involved in this ministry and 5 percentage points more likely to do it frequently. Active deacons working exclusively in parish(es) are 13 percentage points more likely than those not working in parish(es) to be involved in this ministry. Active deacons living in the Northeast are 7 to 9 percentage points more likely than those in the Midwest and the South to frequently engage in this ministry.

About nine in ten active deacons (89 percent) *celebrate Baptisms*; 12 percent do these at least once a week. Active deacons in the two younger ordination cohorts are 5 to 7 percentage points more likely than those who were ordained between 1970 and 1985 to be involved in this ministry. Active deacons who are compensated are 4 percentage points more likely than those who are not compensated to be involved in this ministry. Active deacons working exclusively in parish(es) are 24 percentage points more likely than those not working in parish(es) to be involved in this ministry. Active deacons living in the Northeast are 5 percentage points more likely than those in the South to be involved in this ministry. Active deacons living in the Northeast are 7 to 9 percentage points more likely than those in the Midwest and the South to frequently engage in this ministry.

More than three in four active deacons (77 percent) *officiate at Liturgy of Hours/Exposition*; 14 percent do this at least once a week. Active deacons who were ordained in 2006 or later are 7 percentage points more likely than those who were ordained between 1970 and 1985 to be involved in this ministry. Active deacons who are married are 9 percentage points more likely than those who are not married to be involved in this ministry, but they are 7 percentage points less likely to frequently engage in this ministry. Active deacons working exclusively in parish(es) are 32 percentage points more likely than those not working in parish(es) to be involved in this ministry.

About three in four active deacons (76 percent) say they *preside at Word and communion services in the absence of a priest*; 19 percent do so at least once a week. Active deacons in the two older ordination cohorts are 5 to 9 percentage points more likely than those who were ordained in 2006 or later to frequently engage in this ministry. Active deacons who are compensated are 7 percentage points more likely than those who are not compensated to be involved in this ministry and 5 percentage points more likely to do it frequently. Active deacons not working in parish(es) are 16 percentage points more likely than those working exclusively in parish(es) to frequently engage in this ministry. Active deacons living in the South are 10 percentage points more likely than those in the Northeast to be involved in this ministry.

Three in four active deacons (74 percent) *conduct public rites of blessing or other prayer services*; 8 percent do this at least once a week. Active deacons who were ordained between 1986 and 2005 are 8 percentage points more likely than those who were ordained between 1970 and 1985 to be involved in this ministry. Active deacons who are compensated are 8 percentage points more likely than those who are not compensated to be involved in this ministry. Active deacons not working in parish(es) are 22 percentage points more likely than those working exclusively in parish(es) to frequently engage in this ministry.

Two in three active deacons (66 percent) *witness Marriages*; about half (49 percent) do this a few times a year and only 5 percent report doing this weekly or more often. Active deacons who were ordained between 1986 and 2005 are 7 percentage points more likely than those who were ordained in 2006 or later to be involved in this ministry. Active deacons in the two older ordination cohorts are 4 percentage points more likely than those who were ordained in 2006 or later to frequently engage in this ministry. Active deacons who are compensated are 11 percentage points more likely than those who are not compensated to be involved in this ministry. Active deacons working exclusively in parish(es) are 21 percentage points more likely than those not working in parish(es) to be involved in this ministry.

Ministry of Charity

The diaconal functions regarding charity are very broad and wide-ranging. Those functions tend to focus on promoting and sustaining the apostolic activities of laymen, carrying out the duties of charity and of administration, as well as works of social assistance (Pope Paul VI 1967).

On average, active deacons spend seven hours per week in the ministry of charity (a median of five hours per week). Three in five (61 percent) report one to five hours per week in this ministry and a quarter (24 percent) report six to ten hours per week. The remaining 15 percent of deacons spend more than ten hours per week on the ministry of charity.

The ministry of charity can take many different forms. Figure 5.5 shows the approximate proportion of time that active deacons report spending in

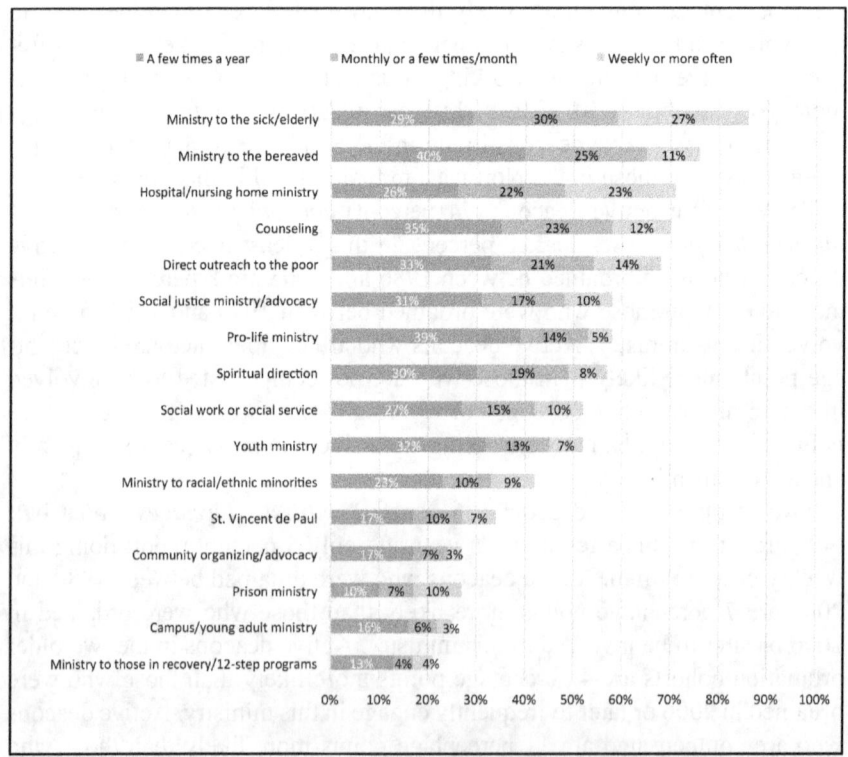

Figure 5.5. Active deacons' involvement in forms of ministry of charity.
Graphic courtesy of the author.

each of these various forms of ministry of charity. The most common among them is *ministry to the sick/elderly*. Ministry to the sick/elderly is reported by 86 percent of active deacons; 27 percent do this ministry at least once a week. Active deacons who are compensated are 6 percentage points more likely than those who are not compensated to be involved in this ministry and 8 percentage points more likely to do it frequently. Active deacons not working in parish(es) are 16 percentage points more likely than those working exclusively in parish(es) to frequently engage in this ministry. Active deacons living in the Midwest are 7 percentage points more likely than those in the South to frequently engage in this ministry.

Ministry to the bereaved is reported by 75 percent of active deacons; 11 percent are involved in bereavement ministry at least once a week. Active deacons who were ordained between 1986 and 2005 are 8 percentage points more likely than those who were ordained in 2006 or later to be involved in this ministry. Active deacons in the two older ordination cohorts are 5 to 7 percentage points more likely than those who were ordained in 2006 or later to frequently engage in this ministry. Active deacons who are not married are 8 percentage points more likely than those who are married to be involved in this ministry and 9 percentage points more likely to do it frequently. Active deacons who are compensated are 9 percentage points more likely than those who are not compensated to be involved in this ministry and 5 percentage points more likely to do it frequently. Active deacons living in the Midwest and the West are 10 percentage points more likely than those in the Northeast to be involved in this ministry.

Seven in ten active deacons (71 percent) engage in *hospital/nursing home ministry*; 23 percent do this at least once a week. Active deacons who are not married are 7 percentage points more likely than those who are married to frequently engage in this ministry. Active deacons who are compensated are 7 percentage points more likely than those who are not compensated to be involved in this ministry and 5 percentage points more likely to do it frequently. Active deacons not working in parish(es) are 24 percentage points more likely than those working exclusively in parish(es) to frequently engage in this ministry. Active deacons living in the Midwest are 7 to 14 percentage points more likely than those in the other three regions to be involved in this ministry. Active deacons living in the Midwest are 7 to 10 percentage points more likely than those in the South and the West to frequently engage in this ministry.

Counseling is a form of the ministry of charity that 70 percent of active deacons are involved in; 12 percent do it at least once a week. Active deacons who were ordained between 1986 and 2005 are 4 percentage points more likely than those who were ordained in 2006 or later to be involved in this ministry. Active deacons who were ordained between 1986 and 2005 are 4 percentage points more likely than those who were ordained in 2006 or later to frequently engage in this ministry. Active deacons who are compensated are 10 percentage points more likely than those who are not compensated to be involved in this ministry and 11 percentage points more likely to do it frequently. Active deacons not working in parish(es) are 21 percentage points more likely than those working exclusively in parish(es) to be involved in this ministry and 34 percentage points more likely to do it frequently. Active deacons living in the West are 9 percentage points more likely than those in the Midwest to be involved in this ministry.

Two in three active deacons (68 percent) perform acts of *direct outreach to the poor*; 14 percent do this at least once a week. Active deacons who were ordained between 1986 and 2005 are 7 percentage points more likely than those who were ordained in 2006 or later to be involved in this ministry. Active deacons who were ordained between 1970 and 1985 are 7 percentage points more likely than those who were ordained in 2006 or later to frequently engage in this ministry. Active deacons who are compensated are 10 percentage points more likely than those who are not compensated to be involved in this ministry and 5 percentage points more likely to do it frequently. Active deacons not working in parish(es) are 25 percentage points more likely than those working exclusively in parish(es) to frequently engage in this ministry. Active deacons living in the West are 9 percentage points more likely than those in the South to be involved in this ministry and 9 percentage points more likely to do it frequently.

Social justice ministry/advocacy is a form of the ministry of charity that is conducted by 59 percent of active deacons; 10 percent do this ministry at least once a week. Active deacons who were ordained between 1986 and 2005 are 4 percentage points more likely than those who were ordained in 2006 or later to be involved in this ministry. Active deacons in the two older ordination cohorts are 4 to 7 percentage points more likely than those who were ordained in 2006 or later to frequently engage in this ministry. Active deacons who are not married are 6 percentage points more likely than those who are married to frequently engage in this ministry. Active deacons who are compensated are 14 percentage points more likely than those who are not compensated to be involved in this ministry and 7 percentage points more likely to do it frequently. Active deacons not working in parish(es) are 22 percentage points more likely than those working exclusively in parish(es) to be involved in this ministry and 23 percentage points more likely to do it frequently. Active deacons living in the West are 13 to 14 percentage points more likely than those in the Northeast and the South to be involved in this ministry.

Pro-life ministry is engaged in by 58 percent of active deacons; 5 percent are involved in this ministry at least once a week. Active deacons in the two younger ordination cohorts are 2 to 8 percentage points more likely than those who were ordained between 1970 and 1985 to be involved in this ministry. Active deacons not working in parish(es) are 9 percentage points more likely than those working exclusively in parish(es) to frequently engage in this ministry.

Spiritual direction is performed by 57 percent of active deacons; 8 percent do spiritual direction at least once a week. Active deacons in the two older ordination cohorts are 7 to 9 percentage points more likely than those who were ordained in 2006 or later to be involved in this ministry. Active deacons who are compensated are 12 percentage points more likely than those who are not compensated to be involved in this ministry. Active deacons not working in parish(es) are 20 percentage points more likely than those working exclusively in parish(es) to be involved in this ministry and 14 percentage points more likely to do it frequently. Active deacons living in the West are 10 percentage points more likely than those in the Midwest or the Northeast to be involved in this ministry.

More than half of active deacons (53 percent) are engaged in *social work or social service*; 10 percent do this ministry at least once a week. Active deacons who are compensated are 11 percentage points more likely than those who are not compensated to be involved in this ministry and 6 percentage points more likely to do it frequently. Active deacons not working in parish(es) are 24 percentage points more likely than those working exclusively in parish(es) to be involved in this ministry and 18 percentage points more likely to do it frequently. Active deacons living in the West are 10 percentage points more likely than those in the South to be involved in this ministry.

Youth ministry is a ministry of charity that 52 percent of active deacons are involved in; 7 percent do youth ministry at least once a week. Active deacons who were ordained in 2006 or later are 4 percentage points less likely than those who were ordained between 1986 and 2005 to be involved in this ministry. Active deacons who are compensated are 7 percentage points more likely than those who are not compensated to be involved in this ministry. Active deacons working exclusively in parish(es) are 27 percentage points more likely than those not working in parish(es) to be involved in this ministry.

Ministry to racial/ethnic minorities is conducted by 42 percent of active deacons; 9 percent do this ministry at least once a week. Active deacons who were ordained between 1970 and 1985 are 6 percentage points more likely than those who were ordained in 2006 or later to be involved in this ministry. Active deacons who are not married are 7 percentage points more likely than those who are married to frequently engage in this ministry. Active deacons who are compensated are 11 percentage points more likely than those who are not compensated to be involved in this ministry. Active deacons not working in parish(es) are 27 percentage points more likely than those working exclusively in parish(es) to be involved in this ministry and 22 percentage points more likely to do it frequently. Active deacons living in the South and the West are 11 to 20 percentage points more likely than those in the Northeast to be involved in this ministry. Active deacons living in the West are 15 percentage points more likely than those in the Midwest to be involved in this ministry.

St. Vincent de Paul is a ministry of charity that 35 percent of active deacons report; 7 percent are engaged in this ministry at least once a week. Active deacons who are compensated are 5 percentage points more likely than those who are not compensated to be involved in this ministry. Active deacons living in the Midwest and the West are 10 percentage points more likely than those in the Northeast to be involved in this ministry. Active deacons living in the West are 5 percentage points more likely than those in the South to frequently engage in this ministry.

Community organizing/advocacy is engaged in by 27 percent of active deacons; 3 percent do this at least once a week. Active deacons who were ordained between 1986 and 2005 are 2 percentage points more likely than those who were ordained in 2006 or later to be involved in this ministry. Active deacons who were ordained between 1970 and 1985 are 4 percentage points more likely than those who were ordained in 2006 or later to frequently engage in this ministry. Active deacons who are compensated are 10 percentage points more likely than those who are not compensated to be involved in this ministry. Active deacons not working in parish(es) are 20 percentage points more likely than those working exclusively in parish(es) to be involved in this ministry and 14 percentage points more likely to do it frequently. Active deacons living in the West are 11 percentage points more likely than those in the South to be involved in this ministry.

Prison ministry is a ministry of charity that involves 26 percent of active deacons; 10 percent engage in prison ministry at least once a week. Active deacons who are compensated are 4 percentage points more likely than those who are not compensated to be involved in this ministry. Active deacons not working in parish(es) are 43 percentage points more likely than those working exclusively in parish(es) to be involved in this ministry and 36 percentage points more likely to do it frequently.

A quarter of active deacons (25 percent) are engaged in *campus/young adult ministry*; 3 percent do this ministry at least once a week. Active deacons who were ordained in 2006 or later are 7 percentage points more likely than those who were ordained between 1970 and 1985 to be involved in this ministry. Active deacons who are compensated are 8 percentage points more likely than those who are not compensated to be involved in this ministry. Active deacons not working in parish(es) are 6 percentage points more likely than those working exclusively in parish(es) to frequently engage in this ministry.

About one in five active deacons (21 percent) are involved in *ministry to those in recovery/12–step programs*; 4 percent do this ministry at least once a week. Active deacons who were ordained between 1986 and 2005 are 4 percentage points more likely than those who were ordained in 2006 or later to be involved in this ministry. Active deacons who are compensated are 9 percentage points more likely than those who are not compensated to be involved in this ministry. Active deacons not working in parish(es) are 26 percentage points more likely than those working exclusively in parish(es) to be involved in this ministry and 12 percentage points more likely to do it frequently.

CONCLUSION

Deacons around the United States carry out diverse ministries that require considerable amounts of time. While deacons are most visible to parishioners when they are engaged in aspects of the ministry of liturgy and, perhaps to a lesser extent, in aspects of the ministry of word, the hours they spend engaged in ministries of charity and in other ministries is largely unnoticed. This chapter sheds some light on the many and various forms of ministry that are performed by deacons.

In addition to their ministerial work, nearly all deacons have family obligations and many are still working in secular jobs while they serve as deacons. This may put significant strain on the deacon himself and on his family. Chapter 6 explores how this may affect deacons' satisfaction and sense of well-being.

Chapter Six

Is It Satisfying to Be a Deacon?
Measuring Satisfaction among Deacons
Jonathon L. Wiggins

Job satisfaction is a difficult concept to quantify. Definitions can be as simple as whether someone likes his or her job. Those getting more specific can use measures such as the pleasure workers derive from their job, how happy they are with their work environment and salary, and the meaning they find in their work. One of the most widely used definitions in organizational research, however, is that of Locke, who defines job satisfaction generally as "a pleasurable or positive emotional state resulting from the appraisal of one's job or job experiences" (Locke 1976: 1304).

Satisfaction among men serving as Catholic deacons is more complicated than just a positive assessment of one's work. Deacons measure their satisfaction not only through how they feel about the amount and kinds of work to which they are assigned, their work environment, or their financial remuneration, but also through their assessment of the impact of their ministry on others.

Francis and Robbins, who encountered this issue in a study of women deacons of the Church of England, listed some of the ways deacons may find satisfaction. They include "the sense that something worthwhile is being accomplished," "the sense that difficulties are being overcome and solutions to problems are being found," and "the sense of personal growth and development" (Francis and Robbins 1999: 152). Concerning clergy compensation, they noted: "the basic philosophy underpinning the clerical stipend is that clergy should be enabled to live without undue financial anxiety and worry about money" (Francis and Robbins 1999: 152).

In distinction from the women deacons Francis and Robbins surveyed, Catholic deacons typically perform their ministry with no expectation of financial remuneration. In addition, they have not always been treated with respect for their role in the life of the Church, with staff members and parishioners/constituents sometimes not even understanding what their role is supposed to be. For example, some of the deacons responding to a question on the 2017 national survey of deacons that asked them what they would most like to see improved, said:

> *Catechesis of the laity on the vocation and ministry of the deacon as a cleric. It's amazing how little this is understood, even by committed Catholics.*

> *Better understanding and appreciation of the order of deacon as separate and distinct from the order of priest. Better understanding of the munus of the order of deacon by presbyters and laity. We are not here to do the work of priests or to replace priests. A decent living wage, including health insurance, for deacons would also seem to be indicated by considerations of basic human dignity and Catholic Social Teaching. There is a widespread assumption that deacons are married; some of us are celibate, and the important witness provided by celibate deacons is almost never recognized.*

> *Improved relationship with priests, to change those priests who consider deacons second class-citizens of clergy. I have been uninvited to deanery meetings. Out of five pastors, I felt only two included me as part of the parish.*

> *Acceptance and collegiality with presbyterate. Consistency in standards of identity as an ordained deacon; standard clerical attire that would identify us as permanent deacons, distinct from priests. Health insurance offered to deacons serving parishes, unless it is provided through secular employment. Many deacons who would otherwise retire from secular jobs to serve the Church full-time, are bound to secular jobs until they qualify for Medicare.*

> *I think there is a need for more formation in the actual doing of the Sacraments, Mass, and counseling. Also, many practicing Catholics lack an understanding of the Diaconate, and I have been trying to educate them with my homilies and personal interactions.*

> *Improve the relationship between priests and deacons. Priests should help deacons to explain the role of deacons, especially the faculties that they have been given by the bishop and give them the opportunity to serve in those faculties. There are some deacons that never use any of the faculties even though there is a need. Some priests do not believe that the diaconate is a religious vocation.*

> *Enhance the relationship between parish employees and deacons, and educate the parish employees to recognize the status of deacon as clergy rather than a volunteer. Better educate "international priests" with an understanding as to the role of the deacon in the parish.*

CARA's surveys of Catholic deacons have incorporated several measures of satisfaction, including overall satisfaction with their lives as deacons, sat-

Table 6.1. Overall measures of satisfaction among U.S. deacons, 2017.

	"Somewhat" or "Strongly" Agree %	"Strongly" Agree Only %
I am happy in my life as a deacon	98	86
If I had a chance to do it over, I would still become a deacon	97	91
I encourage other men to consider serving as a permanent deacon	95	68

isfaction with their ministry, their families' experiences, how their ministry affects their secular employment, how satisfying they find their work environment, how appreciated they feel by those with whom they minister, and their sense of appreciation from others in the diocese.

Examining three of the most direct measures of satisfaction (see Table 6.1), U.S. deacons report very high satisfaction. Virtually all, 98 percent, agree they are happy in their lives as deacons. Nearly the same proportion (97 percent) say they would still become a deacon if they had a chance to do so again, and more than nine in ten "strongly agree" with that statement. More than nine in ten say that they would encourage other men to consider the diaconate and more than two in three "strongly" agree that they would do so.

In fact, one of these direct measures was used by CARA in a previous study of permanent deacons. The 2001 CARA poll of deacons (Gray and Gautier 2004) asked whether they would become a deacon again if they could. Fully 98 percent of deacons in 2001 agreed they would, nearly identical to the 2017 figure.

DIMENSIONS AND CORRELATES OF SATISFACTION WITH LIFE AS A DEACON

Beyond these three relatively direct measures, however, many other questions ask deacons for their opinion about various facets of their ministry and personal lives. The 2017 survey of deacons asked another seven questions specifically about satisfaction with the diaconate as well as forty more questions about different aspects of deacons' ministry and lives.

For the purpose of analysis in this chapter, we have categorized these questions into three general dimensions of the life and ministry of deacons: current ministry experience, interpersonal relationships and well-being, and diocesan support. We examine deacons' attitudes about various aspects related to these three dimensions of their life and ministry in the following sections of this chapter. Where possible, we also compare their attitudes to those of similar questions asked in the 2001 CARA deacon poll referenced above.

One way to gauge how important those other facets are to deacons' overall satisfaction is to examine how strongly they correlate with the most general measure of satisfaction. The broadest measure of satisfaction that we asked of deacons in the 2017 deacons survey is their agreement or disagreement (on a four-point scale) with the statement "I am happy in my life as a deacon." While correlation does not equal causation (that is, we cannot say definitively that one thing causes another, only that there is a likely relationship between the two) this relatively simple test does allow us to narrow the examination of this very large set of attitudes and focus in on those that appear to be substantially related to being happy with one's life as a deacon (i.e. overall satisfaction with the diaconate).

Altogether, twenty-eight other variables had relatively strong correlations[1] with the statement "I am happy in my life as a deacon." These variables are presented and discussed in each subsection below, following the initial description of deacons' attitudes. For these measures of correlation, the higher the correlation, the stronger the relationship between the two variables. Correlation coefficients that are positive numbers indicate that deacons who agreed with the statement tended also to agree that they are happy with their life as a deacon. On the other hand, a negative correlation coefficient indicates that those who agree with the statement tend to disagree that they are happy with their life as a deacon.

Being happy in one's life as a deacon is strongly and positively correlated with the other two broad overall measures of satisfaction shown in Table 6.1. The correlation between "I am happy in my life as a deacon" and the statement "If I had a chance to do it over, I would still become a deacon" is .454 (Pearson correlation coefficient, two-tailed). Likewise, happiness in one's life as a deacon is correlated with the statement "I encourage other men to consider serving as a permanent deacon" at .294.

SATISFACTION WITH CURRENT WORK ENVIRONMENT

When considering how satisfied deacons are with their current work environment overall, it is noteworthy that more than eight in ten deacons at least "somewhat" agree with each of the statements displayed in Table 6.2. They are particularly likely to report having positive relationships with their parishioners (for those who work in a parish), their fellow ministers, and supervising priests. Among those groups, deacons perceive their strongest

Table 6.2. Satisfaction with current work environment, 2017.

	"Somewhat" or "Strongly" Agree %	"Strongly" Agree Only %
I have a good relationship with the parishioners in my parish	99	87
I am happy in my ministry	97	79
I receive respect from those who minister with me	97	78
I have a good relationship with my supervising priest	91	73
I feel trusted by my supervising priest	90	72
Parish staff members appreciate the role of deacon	90	65
I am afforded adequate autonomy in my position	89	56
I have been placed in a position that matches my skill set	87	59
Priests I work with understand and accept the role of deacons	86	55
I share a common vision with my supervising priest	84	55
Laity/parishioners understand the role of deacons for the most part	81	37

relationship being with their parishioners (87 percent "strongly" agree). As noted in the comments from deacons above, however, they are relatively less likely to "strongly" agree that parishioners or the laity understand the role of deacons (37 percent). Concerning the parish staff members, at least 65 percent of deacons "strongly" agree that they give the deacons respect and appreciate the deacon's role. Regarding their supervising priests, deacons are especially likely to agree that they trust them and work well with them, but are less likely to say they share a common vision with them. Finally, a majority of deacons (56 percent to 59 percent) "strongly agree" they are satisfied with the autonomy they are afforded in their positions and that their position matches their skill set.

Ordination cohorts differ for some of these measures. Almost half of those ordained in 1985 or earlier (48 percent) "strongly" agree that laity/parishioners understand the role of deacons for the most part, compared to 39 percent among those ordained between 1986 and 2005 and 33 percent among those ordained in 2006 or later. This suggests that deacons ordained more recently are finding parishioners *less* aware of the role of deacons than those deacons who were ordained years ago, when the diaconate was a new feature of parish life.

Four of the questions in Table 6.2 were also asked, with slightly altered wording, in the 2001 CARA poll of deacons.

- Nearly all deacons responding to the 2001 Deacon poll (97 percent) agreed they had a good relationship with their supervising priest (compared to 91 percent in the current survey), a slight (but not statistically significant) decrease over the past 16 years.
- More than eight in ten deacons in the 2001 Deacon poll (82 percent) agreed that they are satisfied in their ministry (compared to 97 percent in the 2017 survey). This suggests that deacons, on the whole, are even more satisfied in their ministry now than they were 16 years ago.
- More than three in four deacons responding to the 2001 poll (78 percent) agreed that priests understand and accept the role of deacons[2] (compared to 86 percent in the current survey). This represents an increase in agreement over the past 16 years, although the difference in question wording could account for this difference.
- More than eight in ten deacons responding to the 2001 poll (82 percent) agreed that the laity understand and accept the role of deacon,[3] compared to 81 percent in the current survey. There has been no change over the past 16 years in this measure.

Correlations with Overall Satisfaction

Perhaps not surprisingly, the work environment factor that is most strongly correlated with happiness with life as a deacon is "I am happy in my ministry" (Table 6.3). This is a very strong, positive correlation, suggesting that happiness with one's ministry is a large component of being happy with one's life as a deacon.

Table 6.3. Correlating happiness with life as a deacon with current work environment, 2017.

	Correlation Coefficient (r)
I am happy in my ministry	.730
I feel trusted by my supervising priest	.310
I have a good relationship with my supervising priest	.305
I have been placed in a position that matches my skill set	.301
Priests I work with understand and accept the role of deacons	.290
I share a common vision with my supervising priest	.286
I receive respect from those who minister with me	.275
I am afforded adequate autonomy in my position	.274
I have a good relationship with the parishioners in my parish	.262
Parish staff members appreciate the role of deacon	.245
Laity/parishioners understand the role of deacons for the most part	.212

Other aspects of the work environment that are strongly correlated with overall satisfaction include several aspects of the relationship between the deacon and his supervising priest, work/life aspects such as autonomy and respect, and aspects of the relationship between the deacon and the parish staff and parishioners. Of those aspects, the strongest correlations are related to the relationship between the deacon and his supervising priest (ranging from .310 to .286). Aspects of the relationship between the deacon and parish staff and parishioners are not as strongly correlated, ranging from .262 to .212.

Comments from the open-ended question on the Deacon's survey that asked deacons about what they would most like to see improved also suggest that the relationship between supervising priest and deacon is key to deacons' satisfaction with their work, as can be seen in these comments.

I retired from parish ministry because my last pastor was ignorant of my diaconal role and refused to accept my "outside the parish" ministries of service in hospitals, jails, prisons, nursing homes, and a food pantry.

Some priests/pastors have no use or appreciation for deacons. Thus, they do not tend to use deacons except in things that they do not wish to do or only as a last resort. Many pastors do not want or have time to spend with their deacons to develop an effective team approach to parish needs.

A better acceptance of diaconate ministry by priests (in general) so that we are perceived as partners in ministry not competitors. An improved sense of comradery would help promote mutual understanding and commitment to joint ministry.

Another improvement would be in respecting the faculties of deacons across the board and not have it so dependent on the personal opinion of the pastor. I have served with some pastors who have fully utilized all of the faculties that I have while other pastors have limited my ministry due to his personal opinion and not based on ability or performance. Parochial vicars don't seem to face the same challenges as deacons do when it comes to how pastors use the facilities of deacons. For example, in a previous parish, I was heavily involved with marriage ceremonies, baptisms, and giving homilies. It has taken my current pastor over ten years before he allowed me to do a marriage ceremony. I rarely do baptisms or give homilies. He responds by saying that he just forgets to assign me. He also prefers to celebrate Mass without a deacon—which speaks to a lack of understanding how a Mass with a deacon is a full expression of the Church's ministries. And while my bishop is very supportive of deacons and has expressed this to priests, the pastor is still supreme in the parish.

A better relationship between priests and deacons. A deacon's role in a parish depends greatly upon the vision of the pastor. Some priests consider the dea-

con part of the parish staff and include him in staff meetings or other meetings the priest may have. Others simply consider the deacon to be a "liturgical" assistant—someone who is to assist him liturgically. The deacon is not included in meetings with parish staff other than a parish council meeting.

SATISFACTION WITH THE DIOCESAN ENVIRONMENT

Table 6.4 displays aspects of the deacons' satisfaction with the diocese in which they serve. Between 85 and 90 percent of deacons express satisfaction with their bishop's support of the permanent diaconate and their relationship with him. Communication from the diocese is also well reviewed.

Table 6.4. Satisfaction with the diocesan environment, 2017.

	"Somewhat" or "Strongly" Agree %	"Strongly" Agree Only %
Our arch/bishop is supportive of the permanent diaconate	90	67
I receive communication from the arch/diocese on a regular basis	88	64
The arch/diocese includes me in diocesan functions	88	58
There is a sense of collegiality among the permanent deacons of the arch/diocese	87	49
I have adequate freedom to change the types of ministry I perform in this arch/diocese	86	49
The Office of Permanent Deacons (or similar title) is responsive to the needs of deacons	85	59
I have a good relationship with my arch/bishop	85	50
Deacons are well integrated into the arch/diocese	84	48
I am satisfied with the placement process for deacons in this arch/diocese	84	48
The number of permanent deacons is growing in this diocese	83	49
Morale in the arch/diocese is high among the permanent deacons	80	32
The Office of Permanent Deacons (or similar title) provides an adequate voice for deacons on issues important to them	78	49
I have adequate freedom to change my current ministry site in this arch/diocese	74	34
The arch/diocese includes my immediate family in diocesan functions	62	31
There is a spirit of competition among the permanent deacons of the arch/diocese	18	4

Concerning the inclusion of deacons in diocesan functions, 58 percent of deacons "strongly" agree that the deacons are included, but only 31 percent "strongly" agree that their immediate family is included. Roughly eight in ten agree that the Office of Permanent Deacons in their diocese is responsive to deacons' needs and provides deacons an adequate voice.

Deacons are far more likely to agree that there is a sense of collegiality among deacons in their diocese than to agree that there is a spirit of competition (87 percent compared to 18 percent). The placement process in their diocese is also well received by most deacons (84 percent), with deacons more likely to agree that they have adequate freedom to change the type of ministry (86 percent) than their ministry site (74 percent).

Ordination cohorts display differences on some of these items:

- Sixty percent of those ordained in 1985 or earlier "strongly" agree that they have adequate freedom to change the types of ministry they perform in the diocese, compared to 51 percent of those ordained between 1986 and 2005 and 45 percent of those ordained in 2006 or later.
- Forty-six percent of the earliest ordination cohort "strongly" agree that they have adequate freedom to change their current ministry site, compared to 36 percent of those ordained between 1986 and 2005 and 29 percent of those ordained in 2006 or later.
- Six in ten deacons in the most recent ordination cohort (61 percent) "strongly" agree that the diocese includes them in diocesan functions, compared to 56 percent of the middle ordination cohort and 49 percent of those ordained in 1985 or earlier.
- More than half of the most recent ordination cohort (54 percent) "strongly" agree that there is a sense of collegiality among the deacons of the diocese, compared to less than half (45 percent) of deacons in the two older cohorts.

More recently ordained deacons are a bit younger, have usually had more formal and extended formation, and may be in positions of increased responsibility in the diocese compared to deacons who were ordained many years ago, who may no longer be serving in active ministry. These older, less active deacons may also have more flexibility in choosing their ministry involvement.

Only one of these questions was also asked on the 2001 Deacon poll. In 2001, more than nine in ten deacons (95 percent) agreed they have a good relationship with their bishop, compared to 85 percent of deacons in the 2017 survey. This finding suggests that the overall relationship between deacons and their bishop may have eroded somewhat in the last 16 years.

Correlations with Overall Satisfaction

Not all of the questions relating to aspects of the diocesan environment are correlated with our overall measure of satisfaction, happiness in one's life as a deacon, but among those that are correlated, integration into the arch/diocese and a sense of collegiality have the strongest relationship to overall satisfaction with life as a deacon (Table 6.5).

Other aspects of the diocesan environment that are correlated with overall satisfaction for deacons include the relationship with the arch/bishop, morale among the deacons, and structural support for the diaconate in the arch/diocese. Aspects of the diocesan environment that do not appear to be strongly correlated with overall satisfaction include regular communication from the arch/diocese, inclusion of deacons or their families in diocesan functions, collegiality or competition among the deacons of the arch/diocese, and growth in the number of permanent deacons in the arch/diocese. Comments from the open-ended question on the deacon's survey about what deacons would like to see improved bear out these findings:

> *I would like to see a more embracing and welcoming attitude toward the diaconate by priests and bishops. I am a celibate deacon, and as such am afforded some considerations above that of my married brothers, but that does not mean I am treated any better by sisters, brothers, or priests. Oftentimes the poor treatment comes in the seriousness in which the diocese gives toward diaconate formation and ongoing enrichment. Oftentimes unqualified and unseasoned individuals are placed in offices which are intended to assist dea-*

Table 6.5. Correlating happiness with life as a deacon with diocesan environment, 2017.

	Correlation Coefficient (r)
Deacons are well integrated into the arch/diocese	.251
There is a sense of collegiality among the permanent deacons of the arch/diocese	.246
I have a good relationship with my arch/bishop	.238
Morale in the arch/diocese is high among the permanent deacons	.237
Our arch/bishop is supportive of the permanent diaconate	.231
The Office of Permanent Deacons (or similar title) is responsive to the needs of deacons	.230
The Office of Permanent Deacons (or similar title) provides an adequate voice for deacons on issues important to them	.226
I am satisfied with the placement process for deacons in this arch/diocese	.220
I have adequate freedom to change the types of ministry I perform in this arch/diocese	.210

cons getting training, support, and placement. I have been fortunate that over time I've been able to "win over" my pastors and parish ministers, which has resulted in collaborative working relationship; however, it takes much more work than it ought to.

Acceptance by priests as equals. Most priests seem to only tolerate the deacons assigned to them and at best utilize them in only peripheral ways. I accept that the ministry of the deacon is different, but I do not feel valued by the priests and bishops.

Better relations, respect and cooperation as fellow workers in the vineyard with the pastors of our Diocese. Inclusion and respect as "clergy" with priests and our Bishop.

SATISFACTION WITH INTERPERSONAL RELATIONSHIPS, WELL-BEING, AND SUPPORT

Being happy with one's life as a deacon is also very much related to his sense of personal well-being and the support he receives from those he works and lives with. His happiness also involves his sense that his family supports his life as a deacon and is not negatively impacted by his ministry. Finally, his satisfaction with his life as a deacon is related to his satisfaction with the formation he received for his ministry and his personal history of satisfaction or dissatisfaction with his decision to become a deacon. Each of these aspects of interpersonal relationships, well-being, and support is explored in this section.

Personal Well-being and Support

Satisfaction with one's ministry also has a personal dimension, particularly in regard to the ministry's effect on a deacon's well-being and the personal support he receives (Table 6.6). Among the deacons surveyed, a large majority, eight in ten or more, find sufficient time for personal prayer and have someone they can confide in. At the same time, less than half (44 percent) agree that there is a deacon support group available to them and just a little over a quarter (27 percent) has participated in a deacon support group in the past year.

Three in ten deacons report some difficulty in balancing their home life and ministry, perhaps contributing to the feeling of being burned out that is reported by just over one in ten. About a tenth also report having at least some difficulty living out their promises of obedience and celibacy. The

Table 6.6. Personal well-being and support, 2017.

	"Somewhat" or "Strongly" Agree %	"Strongly" Agree Only %
I have sufficient time for personal prayer in my ministry	95	71
I feel I have someone I can confide in when experiencing issues related to my ministry	79	55
There is a deacon support group available to me	44	22
I have difficulty balancing home life and ministry	31	8
I have participated in a deacon support group in the last year	27	16
I feel burned out in my ministry	13	3
I sometimes have difficulty living my promise of obedience to the arch/bishop	13	3
Honoring my promise of celibacy is a challenge for me sometimes	10	4
My ministry has impaired my advancement in my secular job	9	2

same proportion agrees that their ministry has impaired their advancement at their secular jobs.

Ordination cohorts differ somewhat on these measures of personal well-being and support:

- Eight in ten of the oldest ordination cohort (82 percent) "strongly" agree that they have sufficient time for personal prayer in their ministry, compared to three in four deacons in the middle ordination cohort (75 percent) and 66 percent of those ordained in 2006 or later.
- The oldest ordination cohort is also more likely than the two younger cohorts to agree that there is a deacon support group available to them (56 percent among the oldest cohort, compared to 43 percent among the two younger cohorts).

Correlations with Overall Satisfaction

Just two of these factors having to do with personal well-being and support are correlated with overall satisfaction with one's life as a deacon (Table 6.7).

Deacons who agree that they are happy with their life as a deacon are also likely to agree that they have someone to confide in when they experience issues related to their ministry. At the same time, deacons who are happy with their life as a deacon are likely to *disagree* that they feel burned out in their ministry. Interestingly, having access to a deacon support group or participat-

Table 6.7. Correlating happiness with life as a deacon with personal well-being, 2017.

	Correlation Coefficient (r)
I feel I have someone I can confide in when experiencing issues related to my ministry	.270
I feel burned out in my ministry	-.275

ing in such a group in the past year are not strongly correlated with happiness with one's life as a deacon. At the same time, some of the difficulties of being a deacon—such as balancing home life and ministry, living up to one's promises as a deacon, and conflicts between being a deacon and advancing in one's secular job—are similarly not strongly correlated with happiness with one's life as a deacon.

Family Well-being and Support

A second aspect of the interpersonal relationship and support dimension of satisfaction with one's life as a deacon has to do with the deacon's family relationships. More than six in ten deacons agree that their wife is involved at least "somewhat" with their ministry as a deacon (see Table 6.8). More than nine in ten agree that their wife is supportive of their ministry and that their life as a deacon has strengthened their marriage. On a less positive note, a significant minority of deacons (39 percent) agree that their wife and/or children sometimes feel judged by others as a result of the ministry. In addition, about one in seven deacons agrees that their ministry has put a financial strain on their family.

Deacons ordained in 1985 or earlier (47 percent) are slightly more likely than those ordained later (38 percent in each cohort) to agree at least "somewhat" that their wives and/or children sometimes feel judged by others due to their ministry as a deacon.

Table 6.8. Family well-being and support, 2017.

	"Somewhat" or "Strongly" Agree %	"Strongly" Agree Only %
My wife is supportive of ministry as a deacon	97	86
My life as a deacon has strengthened my marriage	93	68
My wife is involved in my ministry as a deacon	64	35
My wife and/or children sometimes feel judged by others due to my ministry as a deacon	39	12
My ministry as a deacon has put a financial strain on my family	15	5

Correlations with Overall Satisfaction

Just as was the case with personal well-being and support, only two of these questions having to do with family well-being and support are correlated with overall satisfaction with one's life as a deacon (Table 6.9).

Table 6.9. Correlating happiness with life as a deacon with family well-being, 2017.

	Correlation Coefficient (r)
My life as a deacon has strengthened my marriage	.300
My wife is supportive of ministry as a deacon	.257

Deacons who agree that they are happy with their life as a deacon are also likely to agree that their life as a deacon has strengthened their marriage and that their wife supports their ministry. Having one's wife involved in the ministry is not correlated with happiness in one's life as a deacon. Neither are the other two questions about potentially more negative effects of being a deacon—having one's wife and/or children feel that they are judged due to his ministry and feeling financial strain on the family due to his ministry—strongly correlated with happiness with one's life as a deacon.

Personal History with the Diaconate

A final aspect of the interpersonal relationship and support dimension of satisfaction with one's life as a deacon has to do with the deacon's personal experience with the diaconate. In other words, experiences during diaconate formation and regrets about the decision are likely to affect one's overall happiness with life as a deacon.

Table 6.10 displays three questions having to do with deacons' personal history with the diaconate. As can be seen in the table, more than nine in ten deacons agree that their formation and training adequately prepared them for their ministry. Fewer than one in ten deacons even "somewhat" agree that they seriously considered leaving the diaconate in the last five years and even fewer, less than one in twenty, seriously considered leaving in the first five years of their ministry.[4]

Those who have considered leaving the diaconate (but did not do so), either in their first five years of ministry or within their most recent five years, deserve further investigation. Most noteworthy is that 91 percent of deacons who did *not* seriously consider leaving during their first five years also did *not* seriously consider it during their most recent five years. Some 6 percent of deacons did *not* seriously consider leaving during their first five years have since then considered leaving during the past five years. Only 2 percent seriously considered

Table 6.10. Personal history with the diaconate, 2017.

	"Somewhat" or "Strongly" Agree %	"Strongly" Agree Only %
My formation and training adequately prepared me for my ministry	91	46
I seriously considered leaving the diaconate in the past five years	8	3
I seriously considered leaving the diaconate in my first five years of ministry	3	1

leaving both during their first five years and the most recent five years. Finally, 1 percent seriously considered leaving during their first five years but did not leave and have not seriously considered it in the past five years.

The question of how well one's formation and training prepared them for ministry was also asked about on the 2001 poll of deacons. Fully 93 percent of those polled in 2001 agreed their formation and training prepared them for the ministry they have been asked to provide, nearly identical to the 91 percent who said so in the 2017 survey.

Correlations with Overall Satisfaction

The question about the adequacy of formation and training is not correlated with overall satisfaction with one's life as a deacon, but the two questions about consideration of leaving the diaconate are correlated (Table 6.11). Both questions are negatively correlated with satisfaction with one's life as a deacon, indicating that those who seriously considered leaving the diaconate, either in their first five years of ministry or within the past five years, are less likely to indicate that they are happy with their life as a deacon.

Table 6.11. Correlating happiness with life as a deacon with personal history, 2017.

	Correlation Coefficient (r)
I seriously considered leaving the diaconate in the past five years	-.430
I seriously considered leaving the diaconate in my first five years of ministry	-.216

SATISFACTION WITH ASPECTS OF MINISTRY

The 2001 deacon poll asked about areas of satisfaction not covered on the 2017 survey. Deacons' satisfaction in carrying out different aspects of their ministry are shown in Table 6.12. With the exception of administration and

Table 6.12. Satisfaction with aspects of ministry, 2001.

How much satisfaction do you get from:	"Some" or "A Great Deal" %	"A Great Deal" Only %
Assisting at Mass	98	79
Preaching or giving homilies	97	80
Presiding at communion services	96	74
Witnessing marriages	94	71
Pastoral ministry to the sick	93	74
Administration and management	51	16

management, more than nine in ten deacons report deriving "some" or "a great deal" of satisfaction with each aspect. Moreover, between 71 percent and 80 percent say they derive "a great deal" of satisfaction from each. Administration and management is rated considerably lower, with just over half saying they get at least "some" satisfaction from administration and management.

CONCLUSION

Similar to those in other professions, satisfaction with one's life as a deacon is correlated with factors related to satisfaction with elements of the immediate work environment, the larger (diocesan) environment, feelings of interpersonal well-being and support, personal history, and family experiences. Unlike other professions, satisfaction with one's life as a deacon does not appear to be related to their financial compensation or to their level of education.

Examining the areas of their lives where they derive the most satisfaction, deacons on the whole seem most positive about aspects of their work environment, the support of their wives and the impact of the diaconate on their marriage, their relationships and roles in their diocese, and the variety of ministry tasks they are asked to perform. They evaluate some aspects of their work and their work/life balance somewhat lower. Some struggle with their promises to the Church as well as with the effect their ministry has had on their secular jobs and families. The next chapter examines deacons' marriages and family life from the perspective of the wives of deacons.

NOTES

1. Pearson correlation coefficient, r, is a statistical measure of association between two variables. The value of r is always between +1 and -1, and a value of 0 indicates

that there is no relationship between the two variables. Generally, positive or negative values in excess of .2 are considered to be strong enough to be significant.

2. This 2001 question is worded slightly differently than the current question, omitting the words "I work with."

3. This 2017 version of the question adds the word "parishioners" and "for the most part."

4. Of course, it must be noted that some number of deacons who considered leaving the diaconate during their first five years of ministry have already done so and thus were not eligible to participate in this survey.

Chapter Seven

What Does It Mean to Be a Deacon's Wife?

The Diaconate from the Spouse's Perspective

Mark M. Gray

Sociologist Joseph Fichter, SJ noted that deacons are unique among Catholics as they are the only individuals who are likely to receive all seven sacraments (1992: 75). Being both ordained and often married—they may share a life of ministry with a wife and children. At the same time, a 2017 article in *Deacon Digest* about the wives of deacons notes that, "we actually know little about her" (Romanansky 2017: 14). While a number of studies have focused on the diaconate, their wives have less often been studied directly. In this chapter, data on deacons' wives are compiled to present a portrait of the deacon wife from discernment to everyday life in ministry.

AN EVOLVING ROLE

The U.S. Bishops' Committee on the Permanent Diaconate issued the first edition of *Permanent Deacons in the United States: Guidelines on Their Formation and Ministry* in 1971. Some initial expectations are made here with important references about deacon's wives:

- The sacrifice of time during the candidate's formation will have prepared his wife and children for the new dimension and quality that diaconal ministry will bring into their family. It is because of such inevitable changes for the family that the wife must formally consent to her husband's ordination (Bishops' Committee on the Diaconate 1971: §150).
- The deacon's new ministry should be a source of enriched union with his wife. As a member of the Church with apostolic responsibilities herself, the deacon's wife shares her husband's religious concerns and is free to contribute to his new ministry (1971: §151).

- She is not to be an unsalaried, unordained, and unrecognized auxiliary in ministry.... While her help is valued, it must be given in complete freedom; the wife is personally independent of her husband's vocation. For a variety of good reasons, such as her own career or profession or particular needs of her children, the wife may choose not to share at all in the active ministry of her husband (1971: §152).[1]

Thus, it was established that the wife of a deacon is essential to the ministry of a deacon. As a lay person affected by the ordination of her husband, she must provide consent; she may take part in ministry in the Church, but is not obligated to do so.

The National Conference of Catholic Bishops published a national study of the permanent diaconate in 1981, in part to understand the experience of the deacon and his wife in relation to the guidelines. In terms of demography and background, the study concludes, "In general, it appears that the wives of permanent deacons represent a middle-aged, moderately educated group. They report a higher than average number of children, and the majority are still involved in child rearing" (Bishops' Committee on the Diaconate 1981: 27). Half of deacon wives were employed (49 percent). In sum, the researchers note, "a large percentage of wives are involved in both child rearing and employment" (1981: 27).

Despite having many obligations and competing priorities, the study found that deacons' wives who were also involved in ministry with their husband experienced lower levels of stress and higher levels of satisfaction than wives who were not involved in ministry. They conclude, "Overall, the findings indicate a rather high degree of satisfaction among respondents concerning their role as deacons' wives" (1981: 32). They add, "The responses indicate that the wives generally support the permanent diaconate. They feel it has had a positive effect on their own spiritual and religious development, on their relationships with their husband and on their relationships within the Church" (1981: 34).

The guidelines were revised and republished in 1985, given the experience of the early years of the restored diaconate, and included the following aspects related to deacons' wives:

- The married deacons must never lose sight of a practical order of priorities: the sacrament of matrimony preceded the sacrament of orders and thus established a practical priority in the deacon's life. Consequently, he must be able to support his wife and family before he can be acceptable as an ordained minister (Bishops' Committee on the Diaconate 1985: §107).
- The revised *Code of Canon Law* requires the written consent of the wife to her husband's ordination. The consent should be informed consent. For this

reason, it is strongly recommended that the wife of the candidate participate as fully as possible in the entire program of formation (1985: §108).
- There should be opportunities during the course of formation for the wives of candidates to discuss and share their insights, apprehensions, and concerns. These exchanges are most properly coordinated by the wife or a committee of wives (1985: §109).
- The local Church should recognize the rich ministerial potential that may be present in the wives of ordained deacons who have participated in the full formation process, and should they choose to offer themselves in ministry, facilitate the utilization of this potential (1985: §111).

These revised guidelines place marriage and family as the primary sacramental obligation for the deacon. Again, the consent of the wife—this time in writing—is deemed necessary and this is to be informed by the wife's participation, if possible, in the deacon formation program. Here, the wives of deacons are also encouraged to meet and share together in a formal coordinated committee. Given participation in the deacon formation program, wives are also to be strongly considered for ministry roles in the Church.

An updated national study of the diaconate was published by the United States Conference of Catholic Bishops in 1996, which concluded, "The great majority of wives felt involved in their husband's training and continued to feel part of his ministry. Indeed, most of the wives said that they had their own parish ministries" (Bishops' Committee on the Diaconate 1996: 3).

In his 1992 study, Fichter interviewed 109 deacon wives in a U.S. diocese. He finds a demographic profile that is not all that different than the U.S. bishops found in their national study in 1981. He notes some changes over time in formation program participation—namely that formation had become "longer and more elaborate" and that more wives were participating in these programs than did so initially in the 1970s (Fichter 1992: 78). Some of this increased involvement can be explained, according to Fichter, as "the Bishop has not made the attendance of wives mandatory, a certain degree of social pressure is brought to bear on them" (1992: 80). Fichter also finds deacon wives being "regularly encouraged" to take part in ministry with their husband. Yet, he highlights a very common concern among deacon wives as well, "The gender distinction is never so clear as at Sunday Mass, when the husband, in alb and stole, is in the sanctuary while the wife sits alone in the pews" (1992: 83). The women were encouraged to "participate in all liturgical ministries that do not require ordination" (1992: 85), and none of the women Fichter interviewed reported that they had no involvement with their parish. He describes a common role: "they tend to be the 'lay Apostles' of the parish. They are the 'reliables' without whom the parish would lose much of its apostolic effectiveness" (1992: 87).

More recent direction on the roles of deacons and their wives was provided by the U.S. bishops in the *National Directory for the Formation, Ministry, and Life of Permanent Deacons in the United States* in 2005. Here, some focus is given to the role of the deacon and his wife in promoting Church teachings on marriage and family life through ministry and by example:

- "In particular the deacon and his wife must be a living example of fidelity and indissolubility in Christian marriage before a world which is in dire need for such things. By facing in a spirit of faith the challenges of married life and the demands of daily living, they strengthen the family life not only of the Church community but of the whole of society" [quotation from Pope John Paul II's Address to Deacons of the United States on September 19, 1987] (Bishops' Committee on the Diaconate 2005: §67).
- A married deacon, with his wife and family, gives witness to the sanctity of marriage. The more they grow in mutual love, conforming their lives to the Church's teachings on marriage and sexuality, the more they give to the Christian community a model of Christ-like love, compassion, and self-sacrifice (2005: §68).
- The wife of a deacon should be included with her husband, when appropriate, in diocesan clergy and parochial staff gatherings. A deacon and his wife, both as a spiritual man and woman as a couple, have much to share with the bishop and his priests about the Sacrament of Matrimony (2005: §68).

Such is the formal evolution of the role of "deacon's wife." Initially, there was concern expressed about the impact of formation and the demands that the new ministry could have on deacons' marriages and families. There was also the caution that the wife not be viewed as obligated to take part in formation or ministry. After the Church experiences the formation and ministry of the initial classes of deacons and their wives, the guidelines begin to suggest the importance of deacon wives becoming more active and organized within the formation process. Their potential to serve in ministry is also more clearly observed. By 2005, the deacon and his wife are characterized as an essential example to the Church and the broader culture of the sacrament of marriage.

THE DEACON'S WIFE TODAY

More than nine in ten deacons we surveyed are married to a Catholic spouse (Figure 7.1). An additional 2 percent are married to a non-Catholic spouse. Four percent are widowed, 2 percent are single and have never married, and 1 percent has separated from their spouse or is divorced.

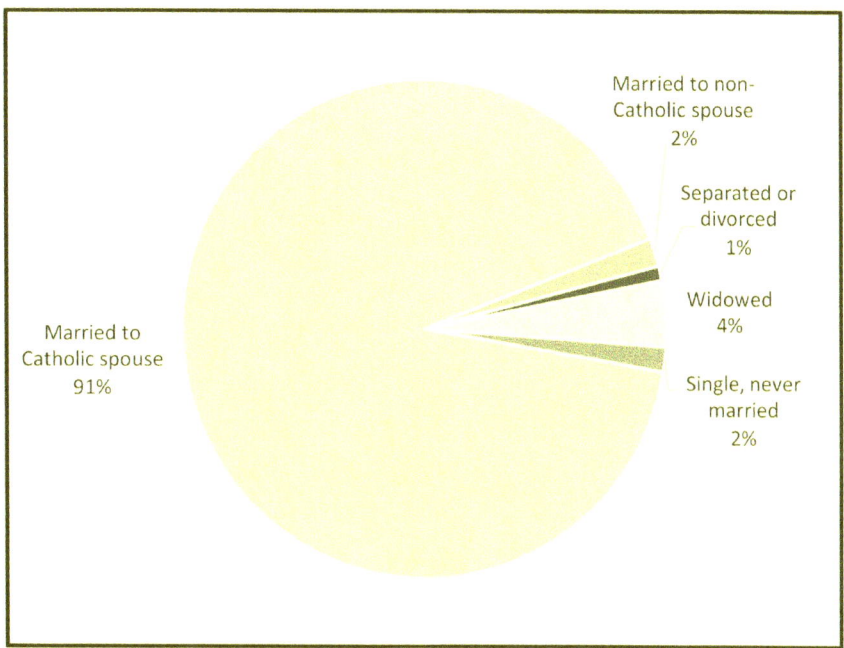

Figure 7.1. What best describes your current marital status?
Graphic courtesy of the author.

Of those who were married when discerning their vocation, 79 percent indicate that their wife was "very" encouraging to them. Sixteen percent said their wife was "somewhat" encouraging. Only one in 20 said their wife was "only a little" (4 percent) or "not at all" (1 percent) encouraging to them while they were discerning becoming a deacon (Figure 7.2).

Today, 86 percent of married deacons agree "strongly" that their wife is supportive of their ministry as a deacon (Table 7.1). Nearly all, 97 percent, agree "somewhat" or "strongly" with this statement.

More than nine in ten deacons agree "somewhat" or "strongly" that their life as a deacon has strengthened their marriage (68 percent agree "strongly" with this statement). Yet, a minority of deacons agrees "strongly" that their wife is involved in their ministry as a deacon (64 percent agree "somewhat" or "strongly" with this statement). Few deacons agree "strongly" that their wife or children feel judged by others due to their ministry (12 percent) or that their ministry has put financial strain on their family (5 percent).

We also conducted two focus groups with deacons' wives. We began by asking them about their husband's discernment and about their involvement in formation. It is important to note that some of these wives experienced this relatively recently, while others did so decades ago. As noted above, much

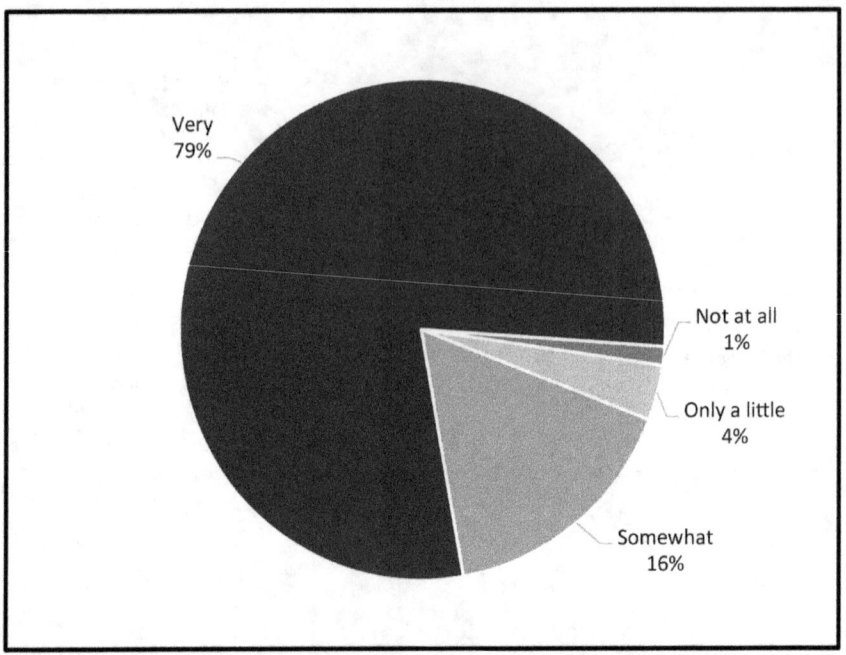

Figure 7.2. While discerning, how encouraging was your wife?
Graphic courtesy of the author.

has evolved for deacon wives since the 1970s. The Church's expectations and visions for the role of a deacon wife have in some ways shifted and expanded.

Many of the deacons' wives did not initially see themselves as fitting into the roles they came to assume. Some express mixed feelings about their husband's vocation and the impact it has had on their relationship and family life. Yet, they see joys and challenges in being a deacon wife and express that these joys help them overcome the challenges.

Table 7.1. Deacons' responses to marriage and family questions.

	Agree "Strongly" or "Somewhat" %	Agree "Strongly" Only %
My wife is supportive of my ministry as a deacon	97	86
My life as a deacon has strengthened my marriage	93	68
My wife is involved in my ministry as a deacon	64	35
My wife and/or children feel judged by others due to my ministry	39	12
My ministry has put a financial strain on my family	15	5

Discernment and Formation

The deacons' wives generally supported their husbands' decisions to consider the diaconate. Many also say they did not have a good understanding of the vocation at that point. They also did not seem to think they fit the role of being a deacon's wife and had some concern about how it would change their marriage and family. In their own words, here are some of their comments from the focus groups:

> *The first thing that I said when [my husband] started talking about the permanent diaconate was actually years before he started formation. Our parish priest had invited him to think about it and he was still too young to start formation. I said, "I am not like any deacon's wife that I know." [laughter] "I don't know how that would work."*

> *He was [first] approached by our pastor. Time went on and another priest and friend approached him and asked him. He started to think about it. . . . So he was really discerning that and he came to me and he said, "What do you think I should do?" I said, "It's okay with me, but it is up to you. It's between you and God." He thought about it and he said, "I think I will do it." So right there I started to think, "What does that mean for me and the family?"*

> *Personally, I didn't think I had a whole lot to do with [the] calling in the beginning. I trusted him, our marriage was wonderful. I said, "Fine, do what you need to do, study what you need to study."*

> *He read a book by St. Francis of Assisi saying "build my Church" and that is what stuck with him because he said, "I want to help my Church. I have never done anything for my Church." So he came home and he said, "You know what? I want to be a parish life director and I need to have a Master's in Theology." He went on, "I am going to apply for that." So he talked to the priest and he told me, "I am going to apply for the diaconate too. What do you think?" I thought to myself, it doesn't really matter because he's been going to school all his life since we have been married and I said, "I will support you with whatever you want to do."*

> *Talk to each other before you start thinking about it. Make sure. . . . I always recommend couples that, if they have little children, I think it is the best time to do it. Because the little children, they are used to being with everybody, having fun with everybody. My daughter was ten. So it was hard for me because she grew up without having us there. Because you have to go everywhere.*

After discerning, the deacon's wives described how they proceeded through the process of application, acceptance, and participation in formation with their husbands. For some, the application process and the period of learning about the expectations of a deacon and his wife included difficulties. Here are two examples:

> *As for the interview and application process, at the time I thought it was very odd that I had to be interviewed, because I wasn't going into the program. I got interviewed by myself when [my husband] wasn't in the room. I thought that was kind of weird, too. And they asked some interesting questions like, "how do you see yourself as Mrs. Deacon?" And my answer was, "I am not Mrs. Deacon and I will never be Mrs. Deacon. I am Mrs. [husband's name] and I will support him in what he does, but I am a separate person." I think that kind of took them aback because they at that time they figured they had two for one. I was kind of surprised that they still let him in.* [laughter]

> *I tell people it was "learn as we go." It wasn't that they didn't tell us the truth—they didn't know the truth. They hadn't lived it long enough to be able to guide us wives as to our expectations. So it was a little scary in that we liked to joke around a lot. We were all pretty much afraid that we were going to do or say something that was going to mess up our husbands' opportunities to be ordained a deacon. Therefore, we all tried very hard to be on our best behavior. That does not lead to being honest when you are in gatherings and also didn't lead to being able to vent and tell what our concerns and problems were because we were afraid if we complained.*

The wives described varying experiences with their husband's formation. All seem to have felt encouragement to attend classes. However, some said they were very involved, while others less so. Some of the factors that appear to have led to less involvement include work, disability, and having young children. Many had very positive experiences in the formation process. Some say it drew them closer together with their spouse and made them realize what a deacon actually is and what they themselves could become in the process. Many also enjoyed being in the community of other men and women going through the process. Representative comments include:

> *As far as going through the classes, he loves to learn, but I was teaching and that is not a nine to five job. So when you go home you still have a lot of work to do. I found that very hard keeping up with classes and working.*

> *We went together to the classes. I did struggle a lot because my daughter was really young and I cried every time and I still want to cry. When we went to class, I had to leave her behind. . . . So that was the struggle I had with going through the diaconate.*

I attended classes with him the first year and intended to do it the second year but the children started to complain, "You are never home." For the second year, I did not attend classes.

We went to all the classes and we were not expected to do the homework of course but I think it was very helpful to be there to understand what is expected of them and how it might affect the family.

The biggest struggle in my husband's class is we did have a couple who had three small children and it was very difficult on them. Because they had to get a babysitter or the wife couldn't come so it was a struggle for them to decide what to do. We also had a woman who wanted to come but because of her disability she was not able to come. There are personal problems in the classes depending on the family situations.

Attend the classes because really you learn with your husband; you grow with your husband. When you are not there, you are not growing together. You don't know what is going on with them.

I think the best part was the community; being around people that shared the same values and the same faith. That was the best part. They are still our best friends today. We had thirty-three and we can still see each other no matter where we are.

CHALLENGES

The wives were asked to describe the aspects of being a deacon's wife that most challenged them. By far, the most common aspects noted are related to marriage, family, and time. While the sacrament of marriage is said to precede the obligations of being ordained, some note tension around how this is experienced in real life. One of the most common challenges noted by the wives is simply having to sit alone during Mass. Others are concerned they are not able to be with family during Christmas or Easter, or when funerals require them to quickly rearrange pre-existing commitments. At the same time, here and in the later discussion of the joys of being a deacon's wife, participants indicate the rewarding nature of people thanking them for "sharing" their husband with them—often for some of the most important moments in their lives.

I always heard that marriage is first but it is not. It's like a three-legged stool. There are three legs—it's marriage, work, and ministry. And they all have to be in balance. So you can't have one better than the other one. You have to have them all in balance and it's going to shift. But as long as you bring it back into balance, that is wonderful.

We had a divorce of a deacon and his wife. The wife listed the Church and the diaconate as the other woman.

Our daughter has had a challenge as well because she lives in [city] so we don't see her on a regular basis. They have always come either to our house or to the in-laws for holidays. When he was first ordained, they came down for Easter and she got a taste of the fact that dad is not there a lot over the Easter weekend and Holy Week. I think she struggled with that because here she comes down and dad's not there. I think she had this struggle and now eight years later they accept it and they come the weekend after or the weekend before.

I can tell you right off, it's the funerals. . . . It's not like every funeral bothers me, but this particular one we had something planned and oops, nope the funeral is here. "Can't you just tell them to delay it a day?" "No, we can't do that." I was really struggling through this particular one. I got there and at the end the one daughter was thanking everyone and was thanking him. Later I was getting ready to leave and she came up to me and said, "I really want to thank you." And I thought, "If you only knew. . . . and I am thinking no you don't want to be thanking me." I said, "He has done all the work." And she said, "No, I thank you because you have given him to us." I can't complain about funerals anymore.

Another difficult aspect of being a deacon's wife relates to changes in how the husband and wife can communicate. Being a deacon creates new "barriers" in that deacons must keep some aspects of their ministry confidential and the wives feel they need to be more cautious in what they say to others. When these matters create stress for their husbands, the deacon wife is unable to help them deal with these pressures at home. In their own words, examples include:

One of the hardest things I had to deal with, especially at the beginning, was the things we could not do together anymore. We had been very involved in a marriage preparation program where the couples came to our house and we had an evening of sharing. When [my husband] was ordained, he was heavily involved preparing couples for marriage. We simply couldn't do that [evenings of sharing with the couples] anymore—it was not appropriate—and there was a great deal he could not share with me anymore. That was hard to accept too, at the beginning. But we got past it.

I know these people; we know everybody in our parish. There is so much confidentiality; so many things that he can't discuss. He will tell me, "So and so came into the office and they told me to tell you 'Hi.'" But the minute he tells me they came into the office I know what that means. It means that he can't tell me anything else, other than the fact that [Name] said "Hi." He can't tell me the fact that he is trying to figure this all out for [Name]. It's that lifetime of sharing with each other. Now all of a sudden he has such a responsibility, and he is keeping the confidences of so many people that we all care about that it's sort of like, "Okay, I understand." But it took me a while to get used to that exclusion, [the feeling that] somebody has got a piece of him that I don't have.

The other thing with the confidentiality is the emotional weight that I see [my husband] carrying in dealing with people in crisis. He is the spiritual director and still does that and so it's been this whole ten years. Sometimes he comes home and he is completely wiped out. It's not something that we can talk about. We may be on the road and he has to pull over because he gets a phone call and he gets out of the car or I get out of the car. It's difficult, but it's a lot to carry.

On a personal level, the deacon's wife also comes to interact with pastors and the bishop in their diocese. The wives explained challenges in communication and scheduling that sometimes arise, creating tension and conflict. However, many also note that adaptation is common and that they develop ways of overcoming these difficulties. Some of the representative comments include:

If he doesn't automatically tell these people, "Let me call [my wife] first," they will remind him, "Did you call [your wife] first?" Because I have had to go down to fight the battles for him so that he isn't the bad guy. So he isn't the one that has to tell the priest "No, I can't do this." He sends me to the office and I have to tell [Father], "[My husband] is stretched a little thin. I don't think he is going to be able to do this, this and this." You have to be that mother, wife, caregiver all the time, because that is what makes them good deacons. They're pastoral and that means they say "Yes."

For me it's not being a very good "no" person when my husband's calendar gets a little full. It has been a huge challenge. He is an extreme extrovert and so to anything asked of him, he says, "Yes, I'll do that, and yes I will do your funeral, and yes I will do the marriage." And pretty soon the calendar gets really full and I am not very good about saying, "Wait a minute, our kids are coming this time." We are still on the balancing act.

What my husband does is when the pastor keeps asking him, he says "Well, I need to ask my wife." That was my big concern; we always take at least one day a week that he doesn't do anything . . . So my husband said that he would never agree to take on more until I talk with you. I like that.

My husband pretty quickly decided to ask me before. So every time the phone rings when it's the bishop he will say, "I will get back to you." And since our children are grown and they don't live around us then he is free to do different things and, like your husband, the bishop calls him more and more.

A group of friends was just sitting around talking about who we thought would be our next pastor. I said, "I think it's going to be [name]," just because I thought it would be him; I really had no idea. Well I got a call from the bishop the next day and he said, "How dare you let the leak out?" So I learned quite quickly that I have to watch what I say, even if it's just to my friends and I had no idea what was going on. Somehow, he found out, so that was a challenge to then remember to always be careful what I say and who I say it to.

One other challenging aspect for wives is their perceptions of how deacons are treated by priests in the diocese and how deacons are included or excluded from events or listings of personnel. Examples include:

In our diocese, we have a bunch of priests who love deacons and a bunch of priests who think deacons are not worth anything.

We had a young priest who was just ordained this past year and he said, "I don't think the ordination of deacons is really a true ordination."

This week we got a new parish directory. My husband is leafing through it page by page. I wasn't paying much attention to that until he said, "Ugh." I said, "What?" and he said, "On the staff page there was a picture of the two priests. One priest with his dog, the financial person and the DRE, and were there any deacons? No!" I was so sad and it really made me mad.

I work on the website for our parish and I remember a few years ago the diocese sent me information about vocations that they wanted put on our website. I sent them back a letter that said I can't in good conscience put this on the website because it does not mention diaconate as an ordained clergy. They said that it [diaconate] is under the lay ministry section. I said, "Well, it belongs with the vocations because it is an ordained ministry. I will not put this on the website because it is giving people the wrong idea."

Parishioners also often don't understand what a deacon is. This can create difficult situations for deacons and their wives. Some parishioners try to go through the deacon to communicate to their pastor. Others do not understand that deacons are volunteers in service to the Church. Here were some of what the wives described:

Someone recently said, "Can I ask you a personal question?" I said, "Yes, what?" "How much do they pay [your husband]?" Deacons don't get a penny for anything. We are fortunate that the funeral homes had built in a stipend so they do get paid for funerals; on occasion they get a little stipend from the families for baptisms but not a whole bunch of people do that. My husband is going to do his first wedding, I don't know if he is going to get a stipend for that from the couple for doing his first wedding. They don't realize that deacons don't get any money from this. Some of them [deacons] have to pay for their own education. We were fortunate that the diocese picks up all the tab to train all the deacons. They just don't realize.

[Interviewer] *Do you think parishioners understand what deacons are?*

[Deacon wife] *Half-and-half.*

[Deacon wife] *Some do and some don't.*

Some think that [deacons] are the watchdog for the priests [that] you have to go through the deacon before you get to the priests. Others use them almost as triage, sometimes our husbands are the triage. Because you [the deacon] have to deal with everything first before you take it to the pastor. Or before you take it to the bishop it has to go through a lot of discussion before the head person who makes the final decision even knows there is a discussion going on because it has to go through your husband first. . . . What my husband always tells them is, "Go talk to Father [Name], go talk to the pastor, what are you talking to me for? I have no decision making on this particular issue."

If they couldn't go to the pastor they would go to my husband like he could just fix everything. They would have meetings constantly and the parishioners wanted to see him to talk about "Maybe you can talk to the pastor about this and this." There were people after Mass that started talking to him and they said, "This needs to be done, and this and this, and you need to say this to the pastor." That was a lot. It's still going on. It was the first year and everybody thought he would fix all the issues that the parish had.

JOYS

Some of the joys most frequently noted by the wives are related to things that may seem initially quite small. Sometimes these come with simple kind comments and gestures from others. Joy is found also in the little things the couples do to recognize each other. Some note that becoming a deacon changed their husband and their marriage in unanticipated, positive ways. Representative comments about the joys of being a deacon wife include:

I think that one of the joys is when people say, "Thank you so much for sharing him with us."

The very first Sunday he was on the altar, our kids were grown and one was married and the other was in college. So I was home alone and so I went to Mass. I walked in and I was looking for someone that we usually sit near. And over to me comes one of the Knights and he put his hand on my arm and said, "[Name], I know this is your first time alone, and I just want to tell you that the Knights are sitting over here and we would love for you to join us." I started crying and everything and that was joyful.

We have a signal between us that he did a good job.

[Response from another deacon wife] *That is so funny, we have a signal too.*

My husband always wanted to sit in the front or the second row and when the kids were little he said "Oh they need to be right up here, so they behave better." I don't know how this all evolved, but I continued sitting in the front pew, so when there is the sign of peace he comes down and he gives peace to the people in the front and second rows and he gives me a kiss. Now people will say "I don't get a kiss!" [laughter]

My greatest joy was on the day of ordination: to experience that with my husband and to know that he has become the man that God has called him to be. My children see the same thing.

During formation, we talked a lot about communication and how this might affect our family. We pledged to each other that we would communicate. This may sound funny, but I know the minute he was ordained it was like a completely new person communicating with me. He always asks me before he does anything that is different, always. It was like that was part of the ordination; it was this special grace to share with me.

The Bishops' guideline documents outline how the deacon and deacon's wife can and should share in ministries if it is possible for them to do so. Many are living out this call and express that it is a great joy to them. The wives see rewards in all different types of ministries—being there for their parishioners' happiest and saddest moments. They feel the impact they have on the community. In their own words:

We don't do a lot of things together ministry wise, although we have done some talks and things for retreats here and there. I enjoy just being a part of the parish and seeing how he brings the Word alive to the people in the pews. I could be out at the grocery store and someone would tell me how much they got out of his last homily. I think that really is a joy for me to see him reach that potential.

With this ministry, God ended up calling me also into his ministry. We have been fortunate because we have been able to work together on the retreat side of things. I find that it's nice to be together with him and spend the time with him. Yes, God called me out of my comfort zone but you meet such great people, so I am really enjoying that part. It brings a lot of joy.

We do visits together in our parish and in the nursing home, which we never did before. To see what that means to the people that we visit is overwhelming. We spend maybe forty-five minutes, sometimes up to an hour with some of them because [we are the only visitors] they have coming. I never thought it would be that rewarding and it's something that we do together. It's your time together and it really means a lot to the ones we visited. And when we leave, they are so grateful. "Oh thank you for coming, we really appreciate it." That has been a big joy for us.

[My husband] has been doing baptisms, preparing couples for getting married, and doing vigils. I enjoy being with my husband doing things together. We have only been married five years. It is just a beautiful ministry and has brought us even closer and to a deeper level so we can grow as a couple.

One of my many joys—there are several—is visiting the sick, which surprised me. I did not have many ministries before I married my husband. In fact, I didn't have any. This man [we visit] is sick and we have had three that have died. Bringing Communion to them, what a privilege! I just feel humbled by that privilege and seeing my husband so good at it. And when we leave the people are saying, "Thank you" and I want to thank them. Because I am receiving much more than what we give.

When the deacon is recognized or asked by one of his own family members for ministry this can also be one of the joys. For example:

A funny part is the grandkids on Holy Saturday. He was walking into the church and he is carrying the candle and the church is dark and really quiet and our two-year-old granddaughter says, "Hi Papa!" [laughter] We have granddaughters and they nicknamed his alb, naturally, as his "dress." He has a black bag that he carries around and it has all his papers and whenever he gets called—he is only in the office one day per week, but he works seven days a week—they call it "Papa's purse." [laughter]

My husband has a black hat and long black coat; he is "Deacon Death." [laughter] That was because the first year—his first permanent assignment—there were quite a few funerals. He took on a few more ministries where he went to the home to talk to the people and to get their stories, and always did the funeral homes, and then the cemetery. The priest would do the Mass and they would work together but [Name] was wearing his black clothes because somebody died. One day my granddaughter said to him, "You know what? Those kids at school told me that you are 'Deacon Death.' What does that mean?" [laughter]

Our daughter got married a year ago and she first said, "Dad will you marry us?" He said, "You know what? I want to walk you down the aisle and I want to be your dad and sit with your mother and I can't do that if I am up there." So then she said, "Well okay." She was friends with our priest and friends with the other deacons so she asked them. And then she asked him to do the homily and he thought, "I should be vested for that," and he struggled with that and asked around. Well, he told her that he couldn't do that because he had to be vested and he wasn't going to go back and change and make a scene. So she all along thought that dad was not going to do this. So the other deacon was doing the wedding and the homily. My husband got up afterwards and spoke, and she had not a clue. The two of them were kneeling and listening, they were talking, and all of a sudden he got up, and they both looked at one another and asked, "What is he doing?" And the first words out of his mouth, both the groom and bride are crying. He was talking directly to them. He didn't want to be vested for that.

A final joy expressed by the deacon wives is in coming to recognize the impact that a deacon has on the broader community. Two examples include:

So my husband being a deacon for [parish] in [city] means that while he is at Mass, while he is in the office or while he is doing the various ministries he is doing, people remember him. We have parishioners who knew him when he was a little boy. We have parishioners who knew him when he was in business. They knew our children and they knew our grandchildren. They knew our parents. This is our hometown. We chose to go away to school but also chose to come back and get married in our home parish, raise our children in our home parish, which is kind of a weird situation. So when I am sitting in my pew and I am watching the people respond to him, when he is doing a homily they are looking at him from a multiple of eyes. . . . But to see people looking at him and realizing that they have known him their whole life. Now he is serving them is what hits me in my heart.

When our new priest came a few years back, he changed the six o'clock Mass every weekday morning, when all the businessmen would go to church before they go to work. He made it a Communion service on Monday through Friday. He told [my husband], "Every morning, you do a Communion service." He [deacon] started doing morning prayer there first before doing the Communion service. People started saying, "What is this thing called Liturgy of the Hours?" So now, he's got about a dozen people who come at 5:45. They do morning prayer with him and then they kick right into the Communion service. All of sudden our pastor is saying, "Maybe I should turn it back into a Mass," because now he's got fifty people going to morning Communion service.... It's like now he is thinking, "Well, maybe I turned over something that I should have kept." All the people are saying, "No, no, no. Keep it. We like it. We do morning prayer, we do a Communion service, and we get off to work." [My husband] makes sure they are all out the door by seven o'clock.

CONCLUSION

Comparing the Church's original vision of deacons' wives to the previous research we have about them, and finally comparing that to the words of these women today, we can see the evolution of this role in the Church with greater clarity. Fichter calls deacon wives the "reliables." This description is still fitting today—perhaps even more so than it was twenty-five years ago.

At the beginning of their journey, these wives often do not see themselves as fitting easily into the role of a deacon's wife. Yet, they are typically very supportive of their husband's call. As time has passed, and the Church has grown in knowledge and modified its expectations, wives are more likely now to be active participants in formation than they were initially—even though this often creates challenges in their lives at work and home. Despite this, the wives express joy in being able to be there in formation with their husbands and often create lasting connections with the other wives and husbands. This community seems to help many of them meet the challenges they may face.

Many see changes in their husband at ordination and soon changes in themselves as well. New challenges arise. That first day, being without their husbands in the pews can be painful. Yet, soon parishioners begin to express thankfulness to the deacon's wife for sharing their husband with them. She begins to share more of herself, in ministry with her husband and often on her own, too. Some of the greatest joys they express are in these moments. Being a deacon's wife also typically involves a balancing act. She is often the person who serves informally as a gateway to the pastor and the bishop as well as to other family members.

In fifty years, the role of the deacon's wife has come into much greater focus. The Church's vision is broader than what was initially described. In some ways the notion of being the "wife of" is the least of it. It's more of a dynamic duo now. To reiterate the now grand vision noted in the *National Directory for the Formation, Ministry, and Life of Permanent Deacons in the United States*, "In particular the deacon and his wife must be a living example of fidelity and indissolubility in Christian marriage before a world which is in dire need for such things. By facing in a spirit of faith the challenges of married life and the demands of daily living, they strengthen the family life not only of the Church community but of the whole of society" [quotation from

Pope John Paul II's Address to Deacons of the United States on September 19, 1987] (Bishops' Committee on the Diaconate 2005: §67).

NOTE

1. The Committee also notes, "Such a clear understanding of the position of a deacon's wife will also be of great benefit in the event that church law changes and women can be ordained deacons. In such cases the women deacon would take on all the responsibilities of ministry, without any confusing comparison with the deacon's wife, who is unequivocally lay" (Bishops' Committee on the Diaconate 1971: §153).

Chapter Eight

Where Do Deacons Fit within the Diocese?

The Diaconate in the Church's Structures

Thomas P. Gaunt, SJ

STRUCTURES OF THE DIOCESE

Although Catholics may most often meet deacons within the context of their parish ministries, the deacon is in service to his diocese at the direction of his bishop. According to the 1985 edition of the Bishops' document that guides the formation and ministry of deacons, "A deacon is ordained for the service of a diocesan Church. Ordained by the bishop, the deacon stands in a direct relationship with his diocesan bishop, in communion with whom and under whose authority he exercises his ministry. . . . It is the bishop who assigns a deacon to a particular ministry" (Bishops' Committee on the Diaconate 1985: §115–16).

Deacons, because of their ordination for the service of the diocese, necessitate a formal structure within a local diocese to support and sustain their relationship with the bishop in terms of their formation, assignment, and supervision. Each diocese has a number of different offices or departments that are responsible for the preparation and ministry of all those who serve in the diocese, such as an Office for Priests, Office for Religious, Office of Lay Ministry, and an Office for Permanent Deacons. The director of each office is appointed by the bishop and is expected to maintain clear and consistent communication with the bishop.

The *National Directory for the Formation, Ministry, and Life of Permanent Deacons in the United States* specifies the appointment of a Director of Deacon Formation and a Director of Deacon Personnel (2005: §266). These two roles are often incorporated into a single Office of the Diaconate within the diocesan structure. The director of both deacon formation and deacon personnel "is to be either a priest or a deacon." (2005: §271 and 286). The formation of deacons and the life and ministry of deacons may be two separate elements under the diocesan director of the diaconate. In dioceses with a large number of deacons such as Chicago, Los Angeles, and Galveston-Houston (each of which has more than 400 deacons) there may be numerous personnel assigned to the Office of the Permanent Diaconate as compared to Lincoln, Wichita, Juneau, Greensburg, Dodge City, Baker, and Jackson, with fewer than ten deacons each.

OFFICE OF THE PERMANENT DIACONATE

In a focus group with bishops, one bishop offered this advice to his brother bishops who may be considering working with deacons, "Number one, have a good director. A really good director—someone who you can basically trust to make the decision about presenting to you a potential candidate."

Nine in ten U.S. dioceses have a Director of the Diaconate or a person with a similar title. Usually, the director is a permanent deacon (72 percent of dioceses have a deacon in this position), but 26 percent of dioceses have a priest in the position and a few dioceses have a lay person as the director. Two-thirds of the directors serve part-time in the position and on average have been in office six years (Gautier and Holland 2017: 49).

Two questions on the 2017 Deacon survey ask deacons about their perception of the Office of Deacons in their diocese. The Office of the Permanent Diaconate is viewed positively by most deacons, with 85 percent agreeing that it is responsive to their needs as deacons, and nearly as many saying that the Office provides an adequate voice for the deacons in the diocese (Table 8.1).

In some dioceses, the Office of the Director of the Diaconate may be divided into two areas of responsibility: the recruitment and formation of deacons (pre-ordination) and the ministry and life of deacons (post-ordination). Chapter 4 dealt in some detail with the formation process for deacons, so we focus here on how the Office of the Permanent Diaconate is structured and how the various responsibilities for recruiting, forming, and supporting deacons are typically managed in U.S. dioceses. The next sections describe

Table 8.1. Deacons' satisfaction with the diocesan office of deacons.

	The Office of Deacons is responsive to the needs of deacons %	The Office of Deacons provides adequate voice for deacons %
Disagree strongly	5	8
Somewhat disagree	10	14
Agree somewhat	26	29
Agree strongly	59	49

how these two areas of responsibility (pre-ordination and post-ordination) are structured in many dioceses.

Director of Deacon Formation

The director of deacon formation reports directly to the bishop and is responsible for deacon aspirants as well as deacon candidate formation. The director often leads a team of people who provide aspects of the formation and advise him on the formation of deacons. It is not unusual for the director, those assisting him, and the faculty all to serve part-time or as volunteers in this ministry. In addition to the formation program faculty, the guidelines also call for a separate director of spiritual formation "who must be a priest" (Congregation for Catholic Education and the Congregation for the Clergy 2002) and who is responsible for "coordinating the entire spiritual formation program" (Bishops' Committee on the Diaconate 2005: §273) as well as a coordinator of pastoral field education (Bishops' Committee on the Diaconate 2005: §275). The guidelines also recommend that the director of deacon formation have advisory boards to assist him with deacon formation policy and with admissions to the diaconate formation program. These advisory boards "should be representative of the pastors, deacons, deacon's wives, religious, and laity" (2005: §281–84).

The particular demands placed on the director of deacon formation can vary widely, depending on how often the diocese offers the deacon formation program and the size of each cohort of deacons. Some dioceses operate their deacon formation program on an ongoing basis, while others gather aspirants into cohorts and then offer deacon formation every two years, every four years, or periodically as the cohort is formed.

Director of Deacon Personnel (Director of Deacon Ministry and Life)

The director of deacon personnel, sometimes referred to as the director for the ministry and life of deacons, is directly responsible to the bishop on matters regarding individual deacons and their families. Among his responsibilities are the ongoing formation of deacons, the supervision (along with others) of the deacons in their ministry, and making appropriate recommendations to the bishop (Bishops' Committee on the Diaconate 2005: §286–89).

Separate directors for the ministry and life of deacons are relatively rare at this time; only one in seven dioceses report having such a position. Usually the Director of the Diaconate has this position. Practically all of the directors are deacons (88 percent) and the rest are priests. Only one-fifth of the directors are full-time, but in the majority of cases (61 percent) this is a paid position within the diocese (Gautier and Holland 2017: 50).

POST-ORDINATION FORMATION

Each diocese is responsible for establishing a post-ordination program of continuing education for permanent deacons that gives due consideration to the deacons' families, secular employment, pastoral demands, and commitment of time. The guidelines recommend that a minimum number of annual continuing education hours should be established. The post-ordination program needs to address the human, spiritual, intellectual, and pastoral dimensions of a deacon's life and ministry (Bishops' Committee on the Diaconate 2005: §241–56).

When asked what advice he would have for a brother bishop, one bishop in a focus group of bishops responded, "The importance of ongoing formation, especially in the spiritual life. In light of the challenges that they are facing in their ministry and the demands placed on them as they have gotten involved [in their ministry]—particularly the demands on their family life—and the blessings and the challenges. But that is not attended to, especially with the importance of retreat availability."

Post-ordination formation is required by nine in ten dioceses and, on average, 21 hours of continuing education is required of deacons each year. Three-quarters of the dioceses offer ongoing formation opportunities for the wives of deacons (Gautier and Holland 2017: 22).

The director of deacon life and ministry is ordinarily expected to coordinate the provision of an annual retreat for the permanent deacons of the diocese. Practically all of the dioceses require an annual retreat for their deacons. Eight in ten dioceses offer a couples' retreat for deacons and their wives, three in ten provide a deacons-only retreat, and one in seven provide a separate retreat exclusively for the wives of deacons (Gautier and Holland 2017: 23–24).

DEACON PERSONNEL BOARD

Just as dioceses have a priest personnel board to assist the bishop in the assignment of priests throughout the diocese to parishes, schools, chaplaincies, and other ministries, so too the bishop may create a deacon personnel board (Bishops' Committee on the Diaconate 2005: §291). Three-quarters of the

Table 8.2. Deacons' satisfaction with placement.

	I am satisfied with the placement process for deacons in the diocese %	I have adequate freedom to change the ministry I perform in the diocese %	I have adequate freedom to change my current ministry site %
Disagree strongly	5	4	8
Somewhat disagree	11	10	18
Agree somewhat	36	37	40
Agree strongly	48	49	34

dioceses have a plan for the placement and ministry of deacons (Gautier and Holland 2017: 51), though these plans are not necessarily developed by the deacon personnel boards.

Overall, the ministry assignment of deacons is well-supported by the deacons themselves, as the great majority of deacons responding to the 2017 Deacon survey report that they are satisfied with the ministry placement process in their diocese (nearly 85 percent). A similar number also believe they have adequate freedom to change the ministry they are engaged in (86 percent), though a slightly smaller proportion report having the freedom to change their current ministry location (see Table 8.2).

DEACON COUNCILS AND DIOCESAN PASTORAL COUNCILS

The creation of a deacon council (or community board) is an option for the bishop and two-thirds of the dioceses have one (Gautier and Holland 2017: 51). The guidelines recommend that the council have elected representatives of deacons and their wives as well as others appointed by the bishop. The council may be given the responsibility for developing a deacon's handbook or policies for approval by the bishop. The council may also assess the ongoing formation and spiritual formation programs provided for the deacons and their wives (Bishops' Committee on the Diaconate 2005: §290).

Additionally, permanent deacons should be participants in diocesan pastoral councils that are created by the bishop (Pope Paul VI 1967: V 24). This participation fits well in the deacon's relationship with the bishop in the exercise of his ministry in the local Church.

DEACON GATHERINGS AND SUPPORT GROUPS

Annual gatherings of deacons for purposes other than retreat are provided by nine in ten dioceses (Gautier and Holland 2017: 23). These gatherings offer the deacons an opportunity among themselves for fellowship and discussion about their ministry.

Additionally, there may be deacon support groups available in the diocese, where smaller groups of deacons regularly meet to share the challenges and graces of their life and ministry. Fewer than one-half of the deacons responding to the 2017 Deacon survey report that a deacon support group is available to them and about one-quarter have participated in a deacon support group in the past year. Although only a quarter of the deacons have participated in a support group, more than three-quarters report that they have someone that they can confide in for issues related to ministry.

IS THE DIOCESE COMMITTED TO THE DIACONATE?

Practically all of the diocesan diaconate directors report that their diocese is committed to calling, forming, supervising, and supporting its deacons (97 percent). A similar proportion feels supported by their bishop. Very few report a lack of commitment or support from the bishop (Gautier and Holland 2017: 46). The deacons responding to the 2017 Deacon survey report having a good relationship with their bishop (85 percent) and agree that the bishop is supportive of the diaconate (90 percent). In some dioceses, deacons have been appointed to key administrative leadership roles. Said one diaconate director, in response to a question about the impact of the diaconate in his diocese, "Deacons hold key positions in the diocese, including Vice Chancellor, Vicar for Deacons, Director of Formation, Director of Life, Ministry and Service for Deacons, and Director of Catholic Cemeteries."

The ministry of deacons is an important part of the day-to-day life of the local Church. The vast majority of deacons believe they are well-integrated into their dioceses (84 percent). They report that they receive regular communications from the diocese and are included in diocesan functions (88 percent). An area that perhaps needs greater attention is the inclusion of the deacon's immediate family in diocesan functions. Nearly four in ten deacons responding to the 2017 Deacon survey report that their diocese does not do this well.

While positive overall in their evaluations, diaconate directors are somewhat less enthusiastic than deacons themselves in their evaluation of how well deacons are understood by parishioners: 76 percent of diaconate directors agree that parishioners understand the role of deacons, compared to 81 percent among deacons nationally. Both groups evaluate the support that deacons receive from parish staffs about the same (91 percent among diaconate directors, compared to 90 percent among deacons), while diaconate directors are a little more positive than deacons nationally in their evaluation of the support that deacons receive from the priests of the diocese (92 percent of diaconate directors agree, compared to 86 percent of deacons).[1] In contrast, diaconate directors are slightly *more* likely than deacons nationally to agree that the diaconate community is supported by the bishop (97 percent of diaconate directors agree with this statement, compared to 90 percent of deacons nationally).[2]

CHALLENGES FOR THE DIACONATE

Deacons receive the sacrament of Holy Orders in their ordination. As such, their life and ministry is governed and ordered in a manner different from lay ministers in the Church. A particular aspect of this attends to the deacon's marriage and family. Specific challenges arise when the deacon's spouse dies or a civil divorce occurs.

Laicization

Once ordained, deacons can be laicized or returned to the lay state by canonical dismissal or because of a dispensation granted by the Holy See (Bishops' Committee on the Diaconate 2005: §99). Laicization is requested by the individual himself or by the bishop of his diocese of incardination. There are numerous reasons or causes for laicization. In recent years about five percent of those ordained are laicized at a later date (Gautier and Holland 2017: 16).

Divorce/Separation

Divorce or separation for a married deacon is a personal and pastoral reality as it is for any other married person. As with other members of the Church, a deacon may petition for a decree of nullity after a civil divorce. In recent years, fewer than 5 percent of deacons experienced a civil divorce during their time of ministry (Gautier and Holland 2017: 16).

Fewer than one-half (46 percent) of the diaconate directors report that their diocese has a formal policy for deacons who are divorced or separated after their ordination (Gautier and Holland 2017: 51). Currently, less than 1 percent of the active deacons in the United States are divorced and not remarried (Gautier and Holland 2017: 12). The few deacons who have experienced a civil divorce typically leave the active ministry or are laicized.

Re-marriage

The current law of the Church is that deacons who are widowed after their ordination as a deacon are expected to remain single. A widowed deacon is not allowed to enter into a new marriage. During their time of discernment and formation, candidates for the diaconate are made aware of their commitment to remain single if they should be widowed in the future. In extraordinary circumstances, the widowed deacon may request that his bishop petition the Holy See for a dispensation allowing him to enter into a new marriage (*Code of Canon Law*: can. 1087 in Bishops' Committee on the Diaconate 1985: §113).

Currently about 4 percent of active deacons are widowed and have not re-married, and less than 1 percent of deacons overall have received a dispensation allowing them to re-marry (Gautier and Holland 2017: 12). The deacons themselves are fairly evenly divided on the question of widowed deacons being allowed to re-marry without a dispensation from the Holy See. More than half (57 percent) agree that widowed deacons should be allowed to re-marry but four in ten (43 percent) disagree, according to the 2017 deacon survey.

WHERE ARE DEACONS GOING IN THE FUTURE?

The permanent diaconate has grown from zero to more than 16,000 active deacons in ministry in dioceses across the nation in the past fifty years. While there are more diocesan priests (25,757 in 2017, according to *The Official Catholic Directory*) than total permanent deacons (19,050 in 2017, according to Gautier and Holland 2017), the numbers who are serving in active ministry is nearly identical, at about 16,000. This fact begs the question, "How many deacons are sufficient for the local Church?" More than four-fifths of deacons responding to the 2017 Deacon survey report that the diaconate is growing in their dioceses.

Two-thirds of the diocesan diaconate directors report there is a need for more deacons in their diocese, and only a third believes their diocese has a sufficient number of deacons (Gautier and Holland 2017: 46–47). Among the deacons themselves, almost half (49 percent) *disagree* that the diocese has enough deacons for current needs. Clearly, the sense among deacons and diocesan diaconate directors is that there is a current and ongoing need for additional deacons in active ministry. Nearly all of the diocesan diaconate directors believe that the diaconate is needed now more than when it was first restored fifty years ago (Gautier and Holland 2017: 46).

The pastoral and ministerial realities of the Church in the United States have dramatically changed over the past fifty years since the restoration of the diaconate and it will continue to evolve in the coming decades. The significant decline in the number of priests and religious available to serve the growing Catholic population is likely to continue into the near future. At the same time, deacons and lay ecclesial ministers are two groups of ministers that are increasing in number in the American Church. Said one diaconate director:

> *As the diaconate matures and evolves, I believe that the Church will find new ways to mine the resources found in our diaconate community. Currently, we are primarily based in parishes and much of our ministry centers on parish life. However, I believe the Church is just now beginning to understand what a resource the diaconate community can be. We have among our deacon community doctors, lawyers, pilots, financiers, business managers, teachers, social workers, human resource executives, independent business owners, psychiatrists, factory workers, and farmers—just to name a few. The wealth of the skills and knowledge of these men has yet to be fully mined by the Church. It is my belief, as the Church begins realizing the potential of its deacons and makes more use of these resources that the best is yet to come.*

Two important social forces have affected and will continue to influence the ordinary day-to-day pastoral reality of parishes and dioceses: first, immigration of Catholics to the United States and the mobility of Catholics within the country; and second, the increasing cultural and ethnic diversity of the Catholic community. These forces have created new pastoral demands upon the local Church in responding to explosive growth in the South and West, how to welcome and include new populations of Catholics into existing parishes, and how to pastorally engage a diversity of cultural communities. The ministry of deacons can be a critical part of the Church's response.

Deacons will have a more visible role of leadership in parishes as dioceses adapt to having fewer priests to serve an ever-growing and diverse Catholic community in the United States. Numerous diaconate directors see a growing need for deacons to serve as parish administers and coordinators. Among their many observations were:

> *I believe permanent deacons may be asked to serve more and more as pastoral administrators.*

> *With the critical shortage of vocations to the priesthood in our diocese for the foreseeable future, deacons will be called upon more and more to take on active leadership roles including that of parish administrator in order to meet the pastoral needs of the faithful. Hence, more work will need to be done to improve the collaboration among clergy.*

The growing cultural and ethnic diversity of the Catholic population in the United States will continue to present ministerial opportunities and challenges for the assignment of deacons. As one director of the diaconate stated, the diaconate needs to be "responding in a very real way to the multiculturization of the Catholic Church in the United States." Currently the active deacons and those in formation are a little more ethnically and culturally representative of the Catholic community than are diocesan and religious priests, as described in chapter 3.

The areas of ministry for deacons likely will continue to increase, particularly in service to those who are on the margins or forgotten. This was expressed by one diaconate director:

> *I see a greater need for deacons in the market places of America and speaking out on the Church's teachings. [Deacons could be] spreading the Gospel and speaking out on issues at the city council level regarding the homeless, veterans, the poor and those living on the edges of society. [Deacons could be serving] as it were "the voice of Christ."*

In 2016, Pope Francis established a Commission for the Study of Women in the Diaconate. The Commission is currently in the midst of its investigation and has not yet issued any report or recommendations to the Holy Father. The question of women deacons is not new, as the 1971 *Permanent Deacons in the United States: Guidelines on Their Formation and Ministry* from the United States Catholic Conference noted, "Among deacon candidates themselves and leaders of training programs, there is growing conviction that women would strengthen the diaconal ministry immeasurably" (Bishops' Committee on the Diaconate 1971: §168). The work of this Commission and the ultimate decision of the Pope in regard to the diaconate may yet transform the diaconate as it begins its next fifty years.

Suggested Improvements for the Diaconate

The deacons of today also have a point of view about the future of the diaconate. The 2017 Deacon survey included the question, "Of everything you have experienced in the permanent diaconate, what would you most like to see improved?" In some cases the responding deacons said "none" or "nothing," likely reflecting their satisfaction with the diaconate in general, and no pressing need for improvements to be made. Among some of the topics they included in their responses to this question, here are some of the most common themes.

Greater recognition of deacons as ordained clergy is desired by some. Representative comments include:

Deacons need to be recognized openly as clergy and given the option to wear clerical collars while in formal ministry, as an outward sign of the Church at work in the world.

Clerics are a sign of ordination. They are worn by bishops and priests as an outward sign to community of their religion. Deacons are not normally forbidden clerics. However, in some areas they are told that civilian attire is the normal wear for them.

Priests helping deacons to explain the role of deacons, especially the faculties that they have been given by the bishop and giving them the opportunity to serve in those faculties.

All deacons in all dioceses should be wearing the Roman collar. This will allow people in hospitals, prisons, funerals, weddings to be able to reach out knowing they are talking with a member of the clergy.

Deacons should have the option of wearing the collar and a grey clerical shirt when we function as Church ministers at wakes, prisons, and hospitals.

A better understanding by all that deacons are clergy.

A desire for improvement in relationships with priests are noted in many comments. Representative responses include:

Pastors should be informed on how to use a deacon and how to integrate him into the parish pastoral plan for parishioners.

I feel that there should be more training of our priests during their formation on the role of the permanent diaconate and how they can be used.

Acceptance of the permanent diaconate by the younger clergy.

Better educate "international priests" with an understanding as to the role of the deacon in the parish.

All pastors should be aware what deacons are called to do—including their role in liturgies.

Improved communication with our pastor and associate pastor.

Don't assign deacons with priests who don't want them.

I would like to see less of an atmosphere of "competition" with priests.

Many priests still do not know what to do with deacons.

A better relationship between priests and deacons. A deacon's role in a parish depends greatly upon the vision of the pastor. Some priests consider the deacon part of the parish staff and include him in staff meetings or other meetings the priest may have. Others simply consider the deacon to be a liturgical assistant—someone who is to assist him liturgically. The deacon is not included in meetings with parish staff other than a parish council meeting.

Some call for more support for deacons—including wages and benefits. Examples of these comments include:

Improved pastoral care for deacons from the bishop. I feel that deacons are treated as a sort of second-class citizen in the diocese. Also, we have special needs because of our marriages and families that fall on deaf diocesan ears.

If we lose our jobs the church is not obligated to help us.

Care for widows of deacons.

Paid mileage.

More funding for National Deacon Conferences.

Increase training in public speaking.

Continuing education.

Diocesan financial support for deacons who do not have sufficient retirement benefits from secular employment and provide significant ministerial services.

Some ongoing evaluation.

Some type of allowance for vestments.

Given more homiletics resources.

Better training in balancing family life with the diaconate.

Some would like to see deacons involved in more or different aspects of ministry. Anointing of the sick is the most frequently mentioned ministry. Representative comments note the following:

I would like to see more deacons in service to the forgotten incarcerated.

In emergency situations I wish deacons could anoint the sick.

More diocesan ministerial or administrative positions set aside for deacons.

I would like to see deacons in hospital ministry receive faculties for the Sacrament of Anointing of the Sick.

A greater emphasis on pastoral care.

Would like to see more deacons in the pro-life ministry.

Anointing and reconciliation.

Deacons involved in mission work.

Deacons should be able to serve as hospital chaplains without having to attend a full chaplain program, as we have had training while in graduate school and/or while in the seminary.

I also think that deacons can and should be assigned as pastoral administrators.

Deacons should be allowed to perform marriages and funerals within Mass.

CONCLUSION

Deacons are an increasingly vital part of the pastoral life of the local Church. The diocesan structures that sustain deacons and their ministry need to develop and grow in personnel and resources to match the greater role of the deacon in today's Church. An important part of this continues to be the education of both the laity and priests as to the role and ministry of deacons. There is also a need for deacons and bishops to foster a better understanding of the personal and pastoral challenges of a married diaconate. How are the ongoing realities of divorce, separation, and re-marriage to be addressed theologically and personally?

The Catholic community in the United States is mobile and increasingly culturally and ethnically diverse. This is both a blessing and challenge for the local Church for which deacons are well suited to respond. The importance of the deacon was well expressed almost fifty years ago by the U.S. Bishops' Committee on the Permanent Diaconate (1971: §28–29).

The deacon must therefore not only listen to the concerns of the community and recognize its feelings and values; he must allow himself to be sensitized by these cultural realities. . . . The motivation for such ministry is fidelity to the Kingdom of God and to the community of people, with a profound respect for their genuine interests. The deacon thus makes practical response to Jesus' command, "Love one another as I have loved you."

NOTES

1. Question wording varies slightly on these two surveys, making direct comparison here problematic. Among diaconate directors, the question was worded "The diaconate community feels supported by priests of our diocese" and the question to deacons was worded "Priests I work with understand and accept deacons." Both questions had a four-point response scale from "disagree strongly" to "agree strongly."

2. Question wording varies slightly on these two surveys, making direct comparison problematic. Among diaconate directors, the question was worded "The diaconate community feels supported by our bishop" and the question to deacons was worded "Our arch/bishop is supportive of the permanent diaconate." Both questions had a four-point response scale from "disagree strongly" to "agree strongly."

References

(Church documents are listed under the name of the pope that promulgated them)

Anderson, John C., and Larry F. Moore. 1978. "The Motivation to Volunteer." *Nonprofit and Voluntary Sector Quarterly* 7 (3):120–29. https://doi.org/10.1177/089976407800700312.

Athanasius. n.d. "Select Works and Letters." Accessed October 17, 2017. http://www.ccel.org/ccel/schaff/npnf204.xvi.ii.iii.html.

Baker, Thomas. 2006. "The Deacon and Work." In The Deacon Reader, edited by James Keating, 135–45. Mahwah, NJ: Paulist Press.

Barnett, James Monroe. 1995. *The Diaconate: A Full and Equal Order*. Harrisburg, PA: Trinity Press International.

The Bible. 2011. New Revised Standard Version Catholic Edition. New York, NY: Harper Collins.

Bishops' Committee on the Diaconate. 1971. *Permanent Deacons in the United States: Guidelines on Their Formation and Ministry*. Washington, DC: United States Catholic Conference.

———. 1981. *A National Study of the Permanent Diaconate in the United States*. Washington, DC: United States Catholic Conference.

———. 1985. *Permanent Deacons in the United States: Guidelines on Their Formation and Ministry*. Washington, DC: United States Catholic Conference.

———. 1996. *A National Study on the Permanent Diaconate of the Catholic Church in the United States: 1994–1995*. Washington, DC: United States Catholic Conference.

———. 2005. *National Directory for the Formation, Ministry, and Life of Permanent Deacons in the United States*. Washington, DC: USCCB Publishing.

Bishops' Committee on the Liturgy, ed. 1974. *Ministries in the Church: Commentary on the Apostolic Letters of Pope Paul VI Ministeria Quaedam and Ad Pascendum*. Study Text 3. Washington, DC: United States Catholic Conference.

———. 1979a. *Study VI: The Deacon, Minister of Word and Sacrament*. Washington, DC: United States Catholic Conference.

———, ed. 1979b. *The Deacon, Minister of Word and Sacrament*. Study Text 6. Washington, DC: United States Catholic Conference.

Campbell, Frederick F. 2006. "The Impact of the New National Directory for the Formation, Ministry and Life of Permanent Deacons in the United States." In *Today's Deacon: Contemporary Issues and Cross-Currents: The National Association of Diaconate Directors Keynote Addresses, 2005*, 13–29. Mahwah, NJ: Paulist Press.

CARA Catholic Ministry Formation Directory. 1997–2017. Washington, DC: Center for Applied Research in the Apostolate.

CARA Post-Ordination Diaconate Surveys, 2006–2016. Washington, DC: Center for Applied Research in the Apostolate.

Central Office of Church Statistics of the Secretariat of State, ed. 2015. *Annuarium Statisticum Ecclesiae (Statistical Yearbook of the Church)*. Vatican City: Libreria Editrice Vaticanum.

Cheek, Dennis, Michal Kramarek, and Patrick Rooney. 2015. "Charity and Philanthropy." Edited by James D. Wright. *Encyclopedia of Social and Behavioral Sciences*. Amsterdam: Elsevier.

Congregation for Bishops. 2004. *Directory for the Pastoral Ministry of Bishops Apostolorum Successores*. Vatican City: Libreria Editrice Vaticana. http://www.vatican.va/roman_curia/congregations/cbishops/documents/rc_con_cbishops_doc_20040222_apostolorum-successores_en.html#Chapter_IV.

Congregation for Catholic Education. 1992. "Circular Letters Concerning the Canonical Norms Relating to Irregularities and Impediments," February 2, 1992.

———. 1998. *Ratio Fundamentalis Institutionis Diaconorum Permanentium: Basic Norms for the Formation of Permanent Deacons*. Vatican City: Libreria Editrice Vaticana.

———. 2005. *Instruction Concerning the Criteria for the Discernment of Vocations with Regard to Persons with Homosexual Tendencies in View of Their Admission to the Seminary and to Holy Orders*. Vatican City: Libreria Editrice Vaticana. http://www.vatican.va/roman_curia/congregations/ccatheduc/documents/rc_con_ccatheduc_doc_20051104_istruzione_en.html.

Congregation for Catholic Education and the Congregation for the Clergy. 2002. "Joint Study of the US Draft Document—*National Directory for the Formation, Ministry and Life of Permanent Deacons in the United States*, Prot. No. 78/2000," March 4, 2002.

Congregation for the Clergy. 1998. *Directorium Pro Ministerio Et Vita Diaconorum Permanentium: Directory for the Ministry and Life of Permanent Deacons*. Washington, DC: United States Catholic Conference. http://www.vatican.va/roman_curia/congregations/ccatheduc/documents/rc_con_ccatheduc_doc_31031998_directorium-diaconi_en.html.

Connolly, R. Hugh. 2010. *Didascalia Apostolorum: The Syriac Version Translated and Accompanied by the Verona Latin Fragments*. Eugene, OR: Wipf and Stock Publishers.

Conway, Daniel. 1992. "The Reluctant Steward: A Report and Commentary on the Stewardship and Development Study." Indianapolis, IN: Christian Theological Seminary and Saint Meinrad Seminary.

———. 2002. "The Reluctant Steward Revisited: Preparing Pastors for Administrative and Financial Duties." Indianapolis, IN: Christian Theological Seminary and Saint Meinrad Seminary.
Coriden, James A., Thomas J. Green, and Donald E. Heintschel. 1985. *The Code of Canon Law: A Text and Commentary*. New York, NY: Paulist Press.
Ditewig, William T. 2006. "Implementation Strategies for the New National Directory of Deacons." In *Today's Deacon: Contemporary Issues and Cross-Currents: The National Association of Diaconate Directors Keynote Addresses, 2005*, 31–53. Mahwah, NJ: Paulist Press.
———. 2007. *The Emerging Diaconate: Servant Leaders in a Servant Church*. Mahwah, NJ: Paulist Press.
Echlin, Edward P. 1971. *The Deacon in the Church: Past and Future*. Staten Island, NY: Alba House.
Fichter, Joseph H., SJ. 1992. "Wives of Catholic Deacons." Chap. 5 in *Wives of Catholic Clergy*. Kansas City, MO: Sheed and Ward.
Francis, Leslie J., and Mandy Robbins. 1999. *The Long Diaconate, 1987–1994: Women Deacons and the Delayed Journey to Priesthood*. Herefordshire, U.K.: Gracewing.
Frisch, Michael B., and Meg Gerrard. 1981. "Natural Helping Systems: A Survey of Red Cross Volunteers." *American Journal of Community Psychology* 9 (5):567–79. https://doi.org/10.1007/BF00896477.
Fuller, Reginald Horace, and Daniel Westberg. 2006. *Preaching the Lectionary: The Word of God for the Church Today*. Collegeville, MN: Liturgical Press.
Gautier, Mary L., Paul M. Perl, and Stephen J. Fichter. 2012. *Same Call, Different Men: The Evolution of the Priesthood since Vatican II*. Collegeville, MN: The Liturgical Press.
Gautier, Mary L., and Jonathon C. Holland. 2017. *A Portrait of the Permanent Diaconate: National Survey of Diocesan Offices of the Permanent Diaconate*. Washington, DC: Center for Applied Research in the Apostolate.
———. 2017. *Catholic Ministry Formation Enrollment: Statistical Overview for 2016–2017*. Washington, DC: Center for Applied Research in the Apostolate.
Gray, Mark M., and Mary L. Gautier. 2004. "Profile of the Diaconate in the United States: A Report of Findings from CARA's Deacon Poll." Working Paper 6. Washington, DC: Center for Applied Research in the Apostolate.
———. 2012. *Consideration of Priesthood and Religious Life among Never-Married U.S. Catholics*. Washington, DC: Center for Applied Research in the Apostolate.
Gray, Mark M., Paul Perl, and Mary L. Gautier. 2008. *Deacons Entrusted with the Pastoral Care of a Parish According to Canon 517.2*. Washington, DC: Center for Applied Research in the Apostolate.
Gunderman, Richard B. 2008. *We Make a Life by What We Give*. Indiana University Press.
Himes, Michael J. 1985. "Models of Diaconal Education." In *Diaconal Reader: Selected Articles from the Diaconal Quarterly*, edited by John F. Kinney, 62–65. Washington, DC: United States Catholic Conference.

Hoge, Dean R. 1994. "Introduction: The Problem of Understanding Church Giving." *Review of Religious Research* 36 (December):101–10.

———. 2002. *The First Five Years of the Priesthood: A Study of Newly Ordained Catholic Priests.* Collegeville, MN: Liturgical Press.

———. 2006. *Experiences of Priests Ordained Five to Nine Years: A Report Published by the Seminary Department of the National Catholic Educational Association.* Edited by Bernard F Stratman. Washington, DC: National Catholic Educational Association.

Hornef, Josef. 1993. *The Genesis and Growth of the Proposal.* Washington, DC: United States Catholic Conference.

Hubbard, Howard H. 1985. "The Vision of Ministering Church." In *Diaconal Reader: Selected Articles from the Diaconal Quarterly,* edited by John F. Kinney, 76–92. Washington, DC: United States Catholic Conference.

Hypher, Paul H. 1985. "The Restoring of Diaconate." In *Diaconal Reader: Selected Articles from the Diaconal Quarterly,* edited by John F. Kinney, 39–46. Washington, DC: United States Catholic Conference.

Ilchman, Warren, Stanley N. Katz, and Edward L. Queen, eds. 1998. *Philanthropy in the World's Traditions.* Bloomington IN: Indiana University Press.

Johnson, Luke T. 2006. "The Life of Faith and the Faithful Use of Possessions." Lecture presented at the Thomas H. Lake Lecture, Indianapolis, IN. http://www.philanthropy.iupui.edu/Lakefamilyinstitute/thomas_lake.aspx.

Kelley, Thomas A. 2008. "There's No Such Thing as 'Bad' Charity." In *Giving Well, Doing Good: Readings for Thoughtful Philanthropists,* edited by Amy Kass, 245–47. Bloomington: Indiana University Press.

Kramarek, Michal. 2016. "Prison Ministry Workers in Indiana." Indiana University—Purdue University Indianapolis. http://gradworks.umi.com/10/00/10009745.html.

Kraus, Theodore W. 1997. *The Order of Deacons: A Second Look.* Oakland, CA.

Kristol, Irving. 2008. "Foundations and the Sin of Pride: The Myth of the Third Sector." In *Giving Well, Doing Good: Readings for Thoughtful Philanthropists,* edited by Amy Kass, 260–67. Bloomington: Indiana University Press.

Kwatera, Michael. 2005. *The Liturgical Ministry of Deacons.* 2nd edition. Collegeville, MN: Liturgical Press.

Libreria Editrice Vaticana. 1983. *Code of Canon Law,* revised edition. Washington, DC: Canon Law Society of America.

Locke, Edwin. 1976. "The Nature and Causes of Job Satisfaction." In *The Handbook of Industrial and Organizational Psychology,* edited by Marvin Dunnette, 1297–1343. Palo Alto, CA: Consulting Psychologists Press.

Murnion, Philip J. 1985. "The Diaconate in the Context of Today's Ministry." In *Diaconal Reader: Selected Articles from the Diaconal Quarterly,* edited by John F. Kinney, 66–75. Washington, DC: United States Catholic Conference.

Noll, Ray R. 2006. "The Sacramental Ministry of the Deacon in Parish Life." In *The Deacon Reader,* edited by James Keating. Mahwah, NJ: Paulist Press.

Olson, Jeannine E. 1992. *One Ministry Many Roles: Deacons and Deaconesses through the Centuries.* Concordia Scholarship Today. St. Louis, MO: Concordia Publishing House.

Orwin, Clifford. 2002. "Princess Diana and Mother Teresa: Compassion and Christian Charity." In *The Perfect Gift: The Philanthropic Imagination in Poetry and Prose*, edited by Amy Kass, 88–101. Bloomington: Indiana University Press.

Payton, Robert L., and Michael P. Moody. 2008. *Understanding Philanthropy: Its Meaning and Mission*. Indiana University Press.

Pope Benedict XVI. 2012. "Apostolic Letter (Issued Motu Proprio) Intima Ecclesiae Natura: On the Service of Charity," November 11, 2012. http://w2.vatican.va/content/benedict-xvi/en/motu_proprio/documents/hf_ben-xvi_motu-proprio_20121111_caritas.html.

Pope St. John Paul II. 1985. "Ai Partecipanti Al Convegno Dei Diaconi Permanenti: Allocution to Permanent Deacons." Vatican City, March 16. http://w2.vatican.va/content/john-paul-ii/it/speeches/1985/march/documents/hf_jp-ii_spe_19850316_diaconi-permanenti.html.

———. 1990. *Codex Canonum Ecclesiarum Orientalium: Code of Canon Law for Eastern Rite Catholic Churches*. Vatican City: Libreria Editrice Vaticana. http://www.jgray.org/codes/cceo90eng.html.

———. 1993. "General Audience on October 6, 1993." Vatican City. https://w2.vatican.va/content/john-paul-ii/it/audiences/1993/documents/hf_jp-ii_aud_19931006.html.

———. 1992. "Post Synodal Apostolic Exhortation on Tthe Formation of Priests in the Circumstances of the Present Day Pastores Dabo Vobis." http://w2.vatican.va/content/john-paul-ii/en/apost_exhortations/documents/hf_jp-ii_exh_25031992_pastores-dabo-vobis.html.

———. 1995. "Deacons Are Configured to Christ the Servant." *L'Osservatore Romano*, December 20, 1995.

———. 1997. *Catechism of the Catholic Church*. Second edition. Vatican City: Libreria Editrice Vaticana. http://www.vatican.va/archive/ENG0015/_INDEX.HTM.

Pope Paul VI. 1964. *Dogmatic Constitution on the Church Lumen Gentium*. http://www.vatican.va/archive/hist_councils/ii_vatican_council/documents/vat-ii_const_19641121_lumen-gentium_en.html.

———. 1965. *Decree on the Missionary Activity of the Church Ad Gentes*. Vatican City: Libreria Editrice Vaticana. http://www.vatican.va/archive/hist_councils/ii_vatican_council/documents/vat-ii_decree_19651207_ad-gentes_en.html.

———. 1967. "Apostolic Letter (Issued Motu Proprio) Sacrum Diaconatus Ordinem: General Norms for Restoring Permanent Diaconate in the Latin Church," June 18, 1967. http://w2.vatican.va/content/paul-vi/en/motu_proprio/documents/hf_p-vi_motu-proprio_19670618_sacrum-diaconatus.html.

———. 1968. "Apostolic Constitution Pontificalis Romani Recognito: New Rite Approved for Ordination of Deacons, Priests and Bishops." http://w2.vatican.va/content/paul-vi/la/apost_constitutions/documents/hf_p-vi_apc_19680618_pontificalis-romani.html.

———. 1972. "Apostolic Letter (Issued Motu Proprio) Ad Pascendum: Norms for the Order of Diaconate," August 15, 1972. http://w2.vatican.va/content/paul-vi/pt/motu_proprio/documents/hf_p-vi_motu-proprio_19720815_ad-pascendum.html.

Rahner, Karl. 1966. "The Theology of the Restoration of the Diaconate." *Theological Investigations* V:268–314.

———. 1974. "On the Diaconate." *Theological Investigations* XII:61–80.

Richardson, Cyril. 1995. "The Letter of Saint Polycarp, Bishop of Smyrna, to the Philippians." In *Early Christian Fathers*, 131–40. New York, NY: Simon and Schuster.

Romanansky, Marcia. 2017. "A Statistical Sketch of the Deacon's Wife." *Deacon Digest*, January 2017.

Searle, Mark. 1985. "Liturgy and Ministry." In *Diaconal Reader: Selected Articles from the Diaconal Quarterly*, edited by John F. Kinney, 93–107. Washington, DC: United States Catholic Conference.

Smith, David Horton, Robert A. Stebbins, and Michael A. Dover. 2006. *A Dictionary of Nonprofit Terms and Concepts*. Indiana University Press.

Sokolowski, S. Wojciech. 1996. "Show Me the Way to the Next Worthy Deed: Towards a Microstructural Theory of Volunteering and Giving." *Voluntas* 7:259–78.

St. Augustine. n.d. "Sermon XXXVI: Homilies on the Gospels." Accessed October 17, 2017. http://www.ccel.org/ccel/schaff/npnf106.vii.xxxviii.html.

St. John Chrysostom. n.d. "Homily LXIII: Homilies on the Gospel of Saint Matthew." Accessed October 17, 2017. http://www.ccel.org/ccel/schaff/npnf110.iii.LX.html.

St. Thomas Aquinas. n.d. "Gospel of Matthew." Accessed October 17, 2017. http://www.ccel.org/ccel/aquinas/catena1.ii.xix.html#ii.xix-p0.1.

Suenens, Leo. 1985. "The Coresponsibility of Deacons." In *Diaconal Reader: Selected Articles from the Diaconal Quarterly*, edited by John F. Kinney, 47–54. Washington, DC: United States Catholic Conference.

Sulek, Marty. 2010a. "On the Modern Meaning of Philanthropy." *Nonprofit and Voluntary Sector Quarterly* 39 (2):193–212. https://doi.org/10.1177/0899764009333052.

———. 2010b. "On the Classical Meaning of Philanthrôpía." *Nonprofit and Voluntary Sector Quarterly* 39 (3):385–408. https://doi.org/10.1177/0899764009333050.

The Official Catholic Directory. 1970–2016. Berkeley Heights, NJ: P.J. Kenedy & Sons.

Thornton, J. P, and S. Helms. 2010. "Afterlife Incentives in Charitable Giving." In *Available at SSRN: http://ssrn.com/abstract*. Vol. 1500662.

Toppe, Christopher M., Arthur D. Kirsch, and Jocabel Michel. 2001. "Giving and Volunteering in the United States: Findings from a National Survey." Washington DC: Independent Sector.

Whitaker, Albert Keith. 2008. "Promethean Legacy: Receptive Giving, Generous Receiving." In *Giving Well, Doing Good: Readings for Thoughtful Philanthropists*, edited by Amy Kass, 206–9. Bloomington: Indiana University Press.

Ziegler, John J. 1985. "Toward a Theology of the Diaconate: Biblical and Early Historical Antecedents." In *Diaconal Reader: Selected Articles from the Diaconal Quarterly*, edited by John F. Kinney. Washington, DC: United States Catholic Conference.

Index

acceptance, 5, 19, 37, 49, 59, 66, 68, 75, 102, 107, 111, 125, 147
active, 7, 18, 35–39, 41–42, 45–49, 57, 59, 61, 65, 70–72, 78, 81–99, 109, 143–44, 146
age, 35, 45–51, 53, 55, *57, 58, 60*, 61, 63, 68, 70–72, 78
Annuarium Statisticum Ecclesiae, 30
anointing of the sick, 148–49
Apostolic Constitution Pontificalis Romani Recognitio: New Rite Approved for Ordination of Deacons, Priests and Bishops, 18
Apostolic Letter Ad Pascendum: Norms for the Order of the Diaconate, 19
Apostolic Letter Intima Ecclesiae Natura: On the Service of Charity, 22
Apostolic Letter Sacrum Diaconatus Ordinem: General Norms for Restoring Permanent Diaconate in the Latin Church, 17, 29
application, 65–66, 125–26
archdeacons, 15
Archdiocese of: Atlanta, 33, *34*; Baltimore, 32; Chicago, 32–33, *34*, 36, 138; Detroit, 32, *34*; Galveston-Houston, 32–33, *34*, 36, 138; Hartford, 32–33, *34*, 36; Los Angeles, 33, *34*, 36, 138; New York, 33, *34*; Newark, 33; Omaha, *34*, 35; Philadelphia, 33, *34*; San Antonio, 32, *34*; Washington, 32, *34*
aspirancy, 66–67
attire, clerical, 102

Baltimore Catechism, 46
Basic Norms for the Formation of Permanent Deacons, 21, 41
bishops, 1–2, 9, 13, 15, 17, 21–22, 29, 37, 39–41, 43, 61, 65, 76, 79n5, 110–11, 121–22, 138, 140, 147, 149

candidacy, 57, 59, 61, 67–68
CARA. *See* Center for Applied Research in the Apostolate
CARA Deacon Poll, xi, 104, 106, 109, 115
Caritas International, 16
Catechism of the Catholic Church, 2, 4, 10, 21
Catholic Charities, 39
Catholic Ministry Formation Directory, 32, 42
Catholic Theological Society of America, 40
Catholic Worker Movement, 26
celibate, 8, 35, 70, 102, 110

Center for Applied Research in the Apostolate (CARA, at Georgetown University), 29, 31, *32*, *36*, 37–39, 41–43, 45, 47, *50*, *51*, *52*, 59, 102–5, 159–60
challenges, 78, 107, 122, 140, 142–43, 146, 149
characteristics, 42–43, 45
Church tradition, 1, 6, 13
Circular Letters Concerning the Canonical Norms relating to Irregularities and Impediments, 22
Code of Canon Law, 9, 18, 20, 39, 120, 144
Codex Canonum Ecclesiarum Orientalium: Code of Canon Law for Eastern Rite Catholic Churches, 20
cohort, ordination. *See* ordination cohorts
Commentary on the Apostolic Letters of Pope Paul VI Ministeria Quaedam and Ad Pascendum, 19
Commission for the Study of Women in the Diaconate, 146
communities, 9, 19, 79n5; black, 9, 19, 79n5; college and university campuses, 9, 19, 79n5; rural, 9, 19, 79n5; Spanish-speaking, 9, 19, 79n5
compensation, 36, 82, 84, 86, 101
conversion to Catholicism, 59
conversion, continual, 71
Council of Nicea, 15
Council of Toledo, 15
Council of Trent, 16
culture, 23, 46, 49–50, 64, 69, 75, 122

Deacon Digest, 119
The Deacon, Minister of Word and Sacrament, 19
deaconesses, 15
decentralization, 7
diakonia, 3–4, 9, 10, 15–17, 21, 23–24, 27n1
Didache, 13

dimensions, formation, 67, 140; human, 67, 140; intellectual, 67, 140; pastoral, 67, 140; spiritual, 67, 140
diocese: Deacon Councils, 141; Deacon Personnel Board, 140–41; Diocesan Pastoral Councils, 141; Director of Deacon Formation, 137, 139; Director of Deacon Personnel, 137, 139; Director of the Diaconate, 75, 137–39, 146; education, continuing, 70, 75, 86, 140, 148; gatherings, annual, 14; Office of Deacons, 39, 138; Office of the Diaconate, 3, 137; Office of Lay Ministry, 137; Office for Permanent Deacons, 137; Office of the Permanent Diaconate, 138; Office for Priests, 137; Office for Religious, 137; policy, formation, 139; post-ordination formation, 70–72, 74, 82, 86, 140
Diocese of: Amarillo, 35; Austin, 33, *34*; Bismarck, 35; Dallas, 33; Des Moines, 32; Duluth, 35; Fairbanks, 33; Gallup, 32; Jefferson City, 35; Knoxville, 35; Lexington, 33, 35; Memphis, 35; Nashville, 35; Peoria, 35; Phoenix, 32, *34*; Rapid City, 35; Richmond, 32; San Diego, 32; Superior, 35; Tulsa, 35
Directorium Pro Ministerio Et Vita Diaconorum Permanentium: Directory for the Ministry and Life of Permanent Deacons, 21
Directory on the Life and Ministry of Permanent Deacons in the United States, 41
Directory for the Pastoral Ministry of Bishops (Apostolorum Successores), 21
discernment, 59, 61–68, 72, 119, 123, 125, 144
Ditewig, William, 7, 16, 18, 30, 79n1, 84
diversity, 48–49, *49*, 145–46
divorce, 54, 122, 128, 143, 149

Index

education, 50, 52–53, 58, 62, 116
employment, 37–38, 53, *54*, 62, 67, 82, 102–3, 120, 140, 148
encouragement, 21, *64*, 64–65, 126
ethnicity, 48–49, *49*
Eucharist, 4, 9, 13–15, 16, 17, 18, 21, 27n1, 90
evaluations, 72, 142

Fichter, SJ, Joseph, 119, 121, 135
financial means, 72
focus groups, 123, 125
formation, 20, 22, 31–33, 40–43, 47, *50*, 52–53, 59–76, 78, 79n1, 79n5, 82, 84–88, 102, 109–11, 114–15, 119, 121–23, 125–26, 132, 135, 137–41, 144, 146–47
functions, 1–6, 8–9, 13–17, 19, 21, 36–37, 86, 90, 94

Garmeen Bank, Bangladesh, 26
Gautier, Mary L., 37, 39, 42, 45, 52, 68, 69, 70, 79nn2–3, 82, 84, 85, 103, 138, 140–41, 142, 143–44
generations: Post-Vatican II, 46, 47, 48, 52, 53, 54, 55, 58; Pre-Vatican II, 46, 47, 48, 51, 52, 53, 54, 55, 58; Vatican II, 46, 47, 48, 52, 53, 54, 55, 58
Gray, Mark M., 37, 39, 52, 79nn2–3, 82, 84, 103

homiletics, 69, 73, 148
homilies, 9, 49, 92, 102, 107, 116
Hull House, Chicago, 26
humanitarianism, compassionate, 24–25

identity, 5, 19, 36, 46, 102
immigration of Catholics to the United States, 145
inquiry, 65–67
Instruction Concerning the Criteria for the Discernment of Vocations with regard to Persons with Homosexual Tendencies in view of their Admission to the Seminary and to Holy Orders, 22
interview, 126
invitation of the Spirit, 5, 19, 37

Jesuit Volunteer Corps, 50, 62
job, secular, 23, 38, 53, 78, 81–82, *82*, 84, 99, 102, 112–13, 116
Josephite Fathers, 32

Kramarek, Michal J., 24, 25, 26

laity, 6, 8, 15, 19, 68, 102, 105–6, 139, 149
leadership, indigenous, 7
leave of absence, 36

marriage, 17–18, *55*, 69, 93, 107, 113–14, 116, 118, 121–25, 127–29, 131, 135, 143–44, 148–40
married, 8, 35, 37, 52, 54, 64, 67, 69–70, 75, 88–89, 92–93, 95–98, 102, 110, 119–20, 122–23, 125, 132–35, 143–44, 149
Mass, 45, 80, 91, 102, 107, 116, 121, 127, 131–35, 149
Mass in English, 46
Mass in Latin, 46
ministerial areas, 4, 19, 86; pastoral service, 4, 19, 86; sacrament, 4, 19, 86; word, 4, 19, 86
ministry: absence of a priest, 18, 93; administration, 9, 18, 22, 39, 86, 94, 115–16; bereaved, 95; Bible study/prayer, 88; campus, *50*, 50–51, 62; community organizing/advocacy, 98; compensated, 37–39, 53, 82, 84–85, *85*, 88–93, 95–99; counseling, 73, 87, 95, 102; education, religious, *50*, 62, 89; evangelization, 87–88; formation, adult faith, 88; hospital chaplaincy, 25, 38; liturgy, 2, 4–5, 8, 13, 16–18, 21, 27n1, 37–38, 69, 81, 86–87, 90–93, 99, 134;

management, 54, 87, 116; military chaplaincy, 85; non-parish, 38, 84; nursing home, 95, 107, 133; outreach to alienated Catholics, 87–88; outreach to the poor, 96; parish, 38–40, 47–49, 54–55, 78, 81, 83–85, 89–99, 102, 105, 107, 111, 121, 137; preparation, baptism, 88; preparation, confirmation, 89; preparation, first reconciliation/first communion, 90; preparation, marriage, 89; presiding at wakes and funerals, 92, 147; prison chaplaincy, 25, 38, 85; proclaiming the Gospel, 91; pro-life, 97, 149; racial/ethnic minorities, 97; recovery programs, 99; retreat, 85, 87, 90, 132–33; schools, elementary or high, 85; sick/elderly, 95; social justice/advocacy, 96; social service, 39, 85, 97; spiritual direction, 69, 87, 97; St. Vincent de Paul, 98; uncompensated, not compensated, 37–38, 78; young adult, 98; youth ministry, *50*, 62, 87

mobility of Catholics, 145

National Directory for the Formation, Ministry, and Life of Permanent Deacons in the United States (Formation Directory), 22, 59, 122, 135, 137

A National Study on the Permanent Diaconate on the Catholic Church in the United States: 1994–1995, 40

A National Study of the Permanent Diaconate in the United States, 40, 120

never-married, 52, 54

norms, 1–2, 8, 17, 19, 23–25, 27, 29, 83

The Official Catholic Directory (OCD), xi, *32*, 33, *34*, *39*, 40, 144

Order of Diaconate, ix, 4

ordination cohorts, 18, 32 40–41, 45, 47–48, *48*, 51–53, 57, *60*, 60–61, 63, 68, 70–71, 84–85, 89–93, 95–97, 105, 109, 112–13, 139

ordinations, 42

permanent deacons, 18, 33, 37, 45, 53–54, *57*, *58*, 60, 78, 79n1, 102–4, 108, 110, 120, 140–41, 144–45

Permanent Deacons in the United States: Guidelines on Their Formation and Ministry, 19, 20, 40, 119, 146

Personal Ordinariate of the Chair of St. Peter, 35

philanthropy, 1, 23–24, 26–27

political parties, 9

Pope Benedict XVI, 22

Pope Paul VI, 2, 3, 5, 6, 7, 8, 9, 12, 15, 17–19, 29, 83, 94, 141

Pope St. Fabian, 14

Pope St. John XXIII, 16

Pope St. John Paul II, 2, 3, 4, 5, 7, 12, 20–21, 23, 67, 86

post-ordination, *36*, 59, 67, 70–72, 74–75, 82, 86, 138–40

preaching, 4, 9, 12–14, 20, 92, 116

pre-discernment, 62

pre-ordination, 59, 61, 69, 72, 74, 78, 138–39

preparation, practical, 74

presbyters, 2, 12–13, 15, 27n1, 76, 102

priests, 2–3, 7–10, 15, 18, 21, 29, 37, 39–40, 45–56, 48, 50, 64, 72, 74–77, 83, 102, 104–7, 110–11, 122, 130–31, 139–40, 143–50

purposes, 1, 8, 37, 71

qualities, spiritual and evangelical, 62

race, 48–49, *49*

Rahner, Karl, 6, 16

Ratio Fundamentalis Institutionis Diaconorum Permanentium: Basic Norms for the Formation of Permanent Deacons, 21, 41

readiness, 62, 66–67

religious orders, 3, 6
re-marriage, 144, 149
restoration, 4, 16, 29, 30, 32, 42, 46, 144; Africa, *30–31*, 31; the Americas, *30–31*, 31; Asia, *30–31*, 31; Austria, 30; Bahamas, 31; Brazil, 30; Canada, 30; Chile, 30; Europe, *30–31*, 31; France, 30; Germany, 16, 30; Great Britain, 30; Iraq, 31; Italy, 30–31; Jamaica, 30; New Zealand, 31; Oceania, *30–31*, 31; Puerto Rico, 31; Sweden, 31; Switzerland, 31; United States, 16, 18, 30–33, *34*; U.S. Virgin Islands, 31
retired, 35–38, *47*, 47–49, *49*, 53, 59–61, 72, 81–82, *82*
retreat, annual, 70, 76, 140
Roman Curia of the Catholic Church: Congregation for Bishops, 2, 4, 5, 21, 86; Congregation for Catholic Education, 4, 10, 21, 22, 41, 65, 67–68, 86, 87, 139; Congregation for the Clergy, 5, 9, 21, 41, 71, 86, 139

sacrament of Holy Orders, 6, 68, 143
sacraments, 8–9, 20, 86, 90, 102
satisfaction, 79, 99, 101–5
schooling, Catholic, *50*, 50–51, *51*, 62
Scripture, 1, 4, 7, 9–12, 17–18, 21, 29, 68, 86
Second Vatican Council, 1, 7, 17, 46–47. *See also* Vatican Council II
service, volunteer, *50*, 62
sisters, 46, 110, 159
Ss. Cyril and Methodius Seminary, 32
suspended, 36, 41

three-fold ministry, 81, 86; charity, 81, *86*; liturgy, 81, *86*; word, 81, *86*
traits, character, 62

U.S. Conference of Catholic Bishops (USCCB), 18, 121; Bishops' Committee on the Diaconate, 4–5, 8, 32, 35–37, 45, 59, 63–64, 66–68, 70–71, 86–87, 90, 120–22, 136, 136n1; Bishops' Committee on the Liturgy, 5, 19; Bishops' Committee on the Permanent Diaconate, 9, 18–20, 22, 40, 79n5, 119, 121
USCCB. *See* U.S. Conference of Catholic Bishops

Vatican Council II: *Decree on the Missionary Activity of the Church (Ad Gentes)*, 17; *Dogmatic Constitution on the Church (Lumen Gentium)*, 17, 19
Vincentian Volunteers, 50
vocations, 63, 65–66, 77, 130, 145

wages and benefits, 148
widowed, 54, 122, 144
wives, 54, 64, 69–70, 76, 78, 113, 116, 119–32, 134–35, 139–41; challenges, 122, 124, 127, 129, 135; consent, 64, 67, 119–21; formation, ongoing, 141; joys, 124, 127, 131, 133, 135; participation, 121, 125; priorities, 120; retreat, 132–33, 140; satisfaction, 120

About the Contributors

Thu T. Do is a Sister of the Lovers of the Holy Cross-Hanoi from Vietnam. She recently finished her doctoral study in Higher Education Administration at Saint Louis University. Her research interests include Catholic higher education, college student formation, and international religious sisters in the United States.

Thomas P. Gaunt is a Jesuit priest and Executive Director of CARA. He has served in Jesuit governance as the Socius/Executive Secretary of the Jesuit Conference-USA and was the Formation and Studies Director of the Maryland and New York Jesuit Provinces. After ordination, he spent ten years as a pastor and as Director of Planning and Research in the Diocese of Charlotte.

Mary L. Gautier is a sociologist and Senior Research Associate at CARA. She specializes in Catholic demographic trends in the United States. She edits *The CARA Report* and other CARA publications. She is co-author of nine books on U.S. Catholicism, most recently *Catholic Parishes of the 21st Century*.

Mark M. Gray is a political scientist and Senior Research Associate at CARA. He specializes in national surveys and trend analysis. He edits the CARA blog, *Nineteen Sixty-four*. He is the co-author of three books, most recently *Catholic Parishes of the 21st Century*.

Michal J. Kramarek is a Research Associate at CARA. He holds a Ph.D. from Indiana University-Purdue University in Indianapolis. His work at CARA ranges from single parish surveys to international multilingual research, combining primary and secondary data as well as qualitative and quantitative methods.

Jonathon L. Wiggins is a sociologist and Research Associate at CARA. He specializes in surveys and pastoral planning for U.S. parishes. He teaches part time in Georgetown University's Bachelor of Arts Liberal Studies program. Recently, he co-authored the 2017 book, *Catholic Parishes of the 21st Century*.

www.ingramcontent.com/pod-product-compliance
Lightning Source LLC
Chambersburg PA
CBHW050140240426
43673CB00043B/1743